★ In Search of Liberty ★

For nearly 100 years the National Society Daughters of the American Revolution has pursued its three objectives (history, education and patriotism) through Service to the Nation. Daughters everywhere strive each day to keep intact the Liberty fought for and won at Lexington and Concord, on the high seas, at New Orleans, at San Juan Hill, in the trenches of Argonne and on the beaches of Normandy and Iwo Jima. Since the inception of the Organization, the Light of Liberty has marked the path of more than 700,000 women striving to perpetuate all that is good and great about America.

From its beginning, NSDAR sought and found many unfulfilled needs throughout the country. One of the greatest needs was the plight of the immigrant. Guided by the Light of Liberty to seek a better life, the newcomer was often confused and frightened upon reaching a strange land. From this great need grew the *Manual of the United States for the Information of Immigrants* (1920). That first edition evolved into the current *DAR Manual for Citizenship* with more than 10,000,000 copies distributed to those preparing for American Citizenship.

Before their final passage through the "Golden Door," it was not unusual for these future Americans to be detained by immigration authorities. The place of detention was usually New York's Ellis Island. Finding this center understaffed and overcrowded, the DAR again saw a need. The detention rooms became the province of the Daughters. They opened new vistas, especially for the women and children, by providing activity, knitting and sewing materials and instructions. The results were so encouraging that the activity, called Occupational Therapy, was introduced into the U.S. Marine Hospital on the Island.

Today, the needs are still evident and the DAR is still fulfilling them: *DAR Manuals* are still distributed; Daughters attend each Naturalization ceremony to welcome new citizens and present Flags.

As Lady Liberty celebrates her 100th birthday, NSDAR at 94, looks on with loving pride and joins her in saying, "God Bless America!"

Flag Day 1984

Sarah M. King

Mrs. Walter Hughey King
President General, NSDAR

IN SEARCH OF
LIBERTY

The Story of the Statue of Liberty and Ellis Island

JAMES B. BELL
AND
RICHARD I. ABRAMS

Doubleday & Company, Inc., Garden City, New York
1984

*For information on how you can help in the restoration of
the Statue of Liberty and Ellis Island, please contact:*

*Statue of Liberty-Ellis Island Centennial Commission
101 Park Avenue — Room 1265
New York NY 10178
(212) 883-1986.*

Library of Congress Cataloging in Publication Data
Bell, James B.
     In search of liberty.
     1. Statue of Liberty National Monument (New York, N.Y.)
— History.   2. Ellis Island Immigration Station — History.
I. Abrams, Richard I. (Richard Irwin), 1934-   .
II. Title.
F128.64.L6B45   1948   974.8'1   83-45554
ISBN 0-385-19624-5
ISBN 0-385-19276-2 (pbk.)
Copyright © 1984 by James B. Bell and Richard I. Abrams

Editorial services and production supervised
by B & W Hutchinson, Inc., Orleans, Massachusetts

Design by Richard C. Bartlett, Penny Darras-Maxwell,
and Cynthia Andrews

Set in 12-point Aster with a Linotron 202
by The Saybrook Press, Inc., Old Saybrook, Connecticut

Contents

Introduction

Five years after President Abraham Lincoln fell
from an assassin's bullet at Ford's Theater—and the fire, smoke,
and smell of war had been stilled at Appomattox—the United States
in 1870 was entering an age of vigorous renewal and development.
Approaching her centennial year, the new nation had survived the
scars and divisions of civil war; it had endured the challenge
and turmoil of impeachment proceedings undertaken against
President Andrew Johnson in the United States Senate; and it was
confronting the dire consequences of the federal government's ill-
considered and ill-fated Reconstruction policies foisted upon the
old Confederacy.

In 1870 the Union's victorious general, Ulysses S. Grant, was
President of the United States. Thirty-nine million people lived in the
nation's thirty-seven states, an increase of over seven million since
the prior federal census in 1860. Four new states had entered the Union
since 1860: Kansas in 1861, West Virginia in 1863, Nevada in 1864,
and Nebraska in 1867.

It was a nation propelling itself in a variety of directions. It
was a land that seemed to enjoy a limitless abundance of resources.
The gold mining frontier, which dramatically drew tens of thousands
to California in the late 1840s had now spread to Nevada, Idaho, and
Montana. For nearly a decade telegraph lines had linked the nation,
from Washington, D.C., to San Francisco, a span westward of nearly
three thousand miles. The business community was in the midst of
a thirty-year scramble to build a network of western railroads; and, on

May 10, 1869, at Promontory, Utah, a golden spike was driven to connect by rail the East with the West under the banners of the Union Pacific and Central Pacific railroad companies. In the East, the New York Central and Hudson River Railroad owned by Cornelius Vanderbilt, and the Pennsylvania Companies' rail network quickly connected the nation's emerging industrial cities.

On the plains from Texas to Kansas and Nebraska, the cattle kingdom was established. Tens of thousands of cattle, driven by cowboys, trekked each year twelve to fifteen hundred miles over the Chisholm Trail, from the Neuces River in east Texas to the Red River crossing, then north through the Indian Territory and on to Abilene, Kansas. The Great Plains was also the scene of fierce conflict between the settlers and the native Americans. United States soldiers and Indian bands fought more than two hundred battles during the seven years from 1869 to 1876. The native Americans were fighting to maintain their hunting rights to long-held territory, while the settlers pressed ever westward seeking new lands for farms, towns, and cities. For the settlers the march was to the Pacific, while for the Indian it was a march to the reservation.

Territorial development and expansion was a mark of the age, too. Alaska, twice the size of Texas, was purchased from Russia in 1867, adding nearly six hundred thousand square miles to the nation's domain. In the West the federal government undertook land surveys, and in 1868 the Wyoming Territory was organized and the first Dakota land boom was underway. Two years later the Texas boom was launched and during the years between 1870 and 1880 the number of Texas farms increased from 61,125 to 174,184.

Mark Twain named the period following the Civil War as "The Gilded Age," minted by the fruits of the new industrial corporations and industry captains. This was the era of the Bessemer process in the manufacture of steel and the establishment of the petroleum industry. John D. Rockefeller founded the Standard Oil Company of Ohio, and Andrew Carnegie ruled the nation's largest steel plants. Inventions also contributed to the dynamic and expansive character of American enterprise: George Westinghouse invented the air brake in 1869; J. W. McCaffey, the suction-type vacuum in 1869; and Thomas A. Edison, the electric voting machine in 1869. The label of "The Gilded Age" was not only an apt description of the new ornaments of personal and corporate wealth, but also a reference to the corruption and weakness in the arenas of local, state, and federal politics.

The literature of the day was really the literature of America's rediscovery of itself following the war between the states. It was the literature of a bold, brash, adolescent nation. Mark Twain, its most famous writer, spoke with the voice of the West, and he won a worldwide reputation for his fervently held American viewpoint, his uncompromising democracy, and his opposition to slavery, snobbery, and chivalry. Mark Twain's style was strong, pointed, and conversational. In his bestseller of 1869, *Innocents Abroad*, he clearly exposed his frontier irreverence for antique culture and traditions.

American painting took on a greater power and resourcefulness, too, following 1865. Two painters, Winslow Homer and Thomas Eakins, stand out in the postwar decade. Homer began as a magazine illustrator for *Harper's Weekly* and came to prominence as a painter in 1866 with *Prisoners from the Front,* a canvas based on his Civil War experience as a pictorial reporter. Thomas Eakins studied at the Pennsylvania Academy of Fine Arts in Philadelphia and the École des Beaux Arts in Paris. In 1869 he traveled to Spain where he was influenced by the style of the earlier painters, Goya and Velásquez. Returning to Philadelphia in 1870, Eakins studied anatomy at the Jefferson Medical College, helping him to become a master of the human figure and resulting in two of his best paintings, *The Gross Clinic* and *The Agnew Clinic.*

Rapid industrialization and new wealth sharply changed older ideas of architecture. Many cities were rebuilt during the generation following the Civil War. Cast iron came into wide use in commercial buildings, and glass in large sheets became available for the first time. New fortunes placed a premium on lavish, glittering design. This was the period also of the first practical passenger elevators, the beginnings of the city office buildings as well as the department store. A French renaissance profoundly influenced American architecture, with mansard roofs and lavish ornamentation used almost exclusively on new public buildings, city brownstones, churches, railroad stations, hospitals, and schools. This style reached its peak in the work of Richard Morris Hunt, designer of many houses for merchant princes in New York City, Newport, Rhode Island, and elsewhere.

A Statue of Liberty

Such was the America that the French sculptor, Frédéric Auguste Bartholdi, observed on his first journey to the United States in 1871: a vigorous, energetic, expansive nation stretching from coast to coast; a nation in the process of change from an agrarian society to a rapidly developing industrial giant; a nation set on harnessing its vast continent and tapping its seemingly limitless resources; a nation that witnessed the rise of cities throughout its great expanse, peopled by men and women from the countryside and from many other lands.

Bartholdi was born on August 2, 1834, in Colmar, a small city in the Alsace region of northeastern France, some thirty miles west of Freiburg, Germany. His father was a civil servant and a substantial landowner. Educated in Paris after his father's early death, Bartholdi spent his summer vacations in Colmar. Not a strong student, he was a painter and put brush to canvas throughout his life. However, his truly keen interest, and the one for which we remember him today, was as a sculptor.

God grant that not only the love of Liberty
but a thorough knowledge of the Rights
of Man may pervade all the Nations
of the Earth, so that a Philosopher may
set his foot anywhere and say,
"This is my country."
               — BENJAMIN FRANKLIN'S PRAYER

Bartholdi's First Visit

Traveling from France by steamship, Bartholdi landed in New York, after a twelve-day sea passage, on June 21, 1871. He was to spend the next five months meeting people and seeing sights from New York to San Francisco.

On his arrival within the Narrows of New York harbor, Bartholdi could see steamships, ferryboats, and church spires from Brooklyn on his right, the skyline of lower Manhattan ahead of him, and the outline of Jersey City to his left. Shortly after docking at a Hudson River pier, Bartholdi recorded his impressions of New York City: a city of people in a hurry, neglected streets, lamp posts of irregular heights, and sidewalk display booths for hawkers of fruits, vegetables, and dry-goods.

When Bartholdi arrived in New York, he knew no one. However, he did carry letters of introduction from friends in Paris to prominent political and literary figures in the United States. He had come to New York as a stranger possessed by an all-consuming passion: For a number of years, Bartholdi had dreamed of building a colossal statue of Liberty in New York harbor. His interest in creating large monuments was not new. In his hometown of Colmar, he had crafted a monumental statue of General Jean Rapp, a local military leader and hero who had served under Napoleon Bonaparte.

★ FRÉDÉRIC AUGUSTE BARTHOLDI. Frédéric Auguste Bartholdi (1834–1904) was born in Colmar, France, and studied painting before turning to sculpture. Throughout his life, his keenest interest was in creating large monuments. Encouraged by French friends who wished to memorialize the long-standing friendship between France and the United States, Bartholdi was very much the spirit and the driving force behind this Franco-American project. The Statue of Liberty is a testimonial to Bartholdi's artistic talents, his persistence in the face of adversity, and his transatlantic diplomatic skills. Many of his other works are located prominently in France and the United States, but by far his most famous monument is the Statue of Liberty.

(Overleaf)
★ NEW YORK HARBOR, ABOUT 1870. This Currier and Ives bird's-eye view shows New York harbor as it appeared during the time Bartholdi first visited the United States in 1871.

12

13

★ LAFAYETTE AND WASHINGTON. This heroic bronze monument by Bartholdi, now located at Manhattan Avenue and 114th Street in New York City, expresses the close personal bonds of friendship and respect between the two Revolutionary War leaders, as well as the historic links between France and the United States.

Years later, Bartholdi recalled the origins of the idea for the Statue of Liberty. It was at a dinner party at the home of the renowned scholar and friend of the United States, Édouard de Laboulaye, some time in 1865. Conversation had turned to the theme of appreciation between nations. While such an attitude did not exist, say, between France and her European neighbors, Laboulaye noted that there would be special links between France and the United States, where the names of the Marquis de Lafayette and the Comte de Rochambeau, priceless allies and leaders for the American cause during the Revolutionary War, were still remembered and held in the highest public esteem. According to Bartholdi, Laboulaye declared: "If a monument were to be built in America as a memorial to their independence, I should think it very natural if it were built by united efforts, if it were a common work of both nations."

The construction of enormous monuments to honor men or nations was not a new idea in 1865. The earliest civilizations erected monuments to honor great men and great ideas. We are reminded of the ancient monuments of Egypt, the pyramids, and the legendary colossus of Rhodes. Bartholdi had seen the pyramids: He had traveled to Egypt in 1856 and again in 1869. During the latter trip he was at work on a plan for a new lighthouse at the entrance to the Suez Canal, whose construction was then being supervised by another Frenchman, Ferdinand de Lesseps. This great lighthouse would stir memories of Alexander's lighthouse at the entrance to Alexandria, one of the Seven Wonders of the ancient world. On his return trip home to Paris, Bartholdi landed in Venice and visited the shores of Lake Maggiore, where he could see the immense statue of St. Charles Borromeo, a sixteenth-century Archbishop of Milan. In that day the statue was one of the world's largest; it was constructed of copper repousse, a thin material worked with a hammer inside and outside and supported internally by iron beams.

In the United States during the mid-1800s, there were two large monuments that had been underway for many years: the Bunker Hill monument in Boston commemorating the famous Revolutionary War battle, which took eighteen years to finish (1825–43), and the Washington Monument in Washington, D.C., whose cornerstone had been laid in July 1848, but remained incomplete until 1884.

★ COLOSSUS OF RHODES. According to popular legend, this towering bronze statue of the sun god Helios stood astride the harbor, with ships passing between its legs. Over 100 feet high and built wholly or in part by Chares of Lindus (Rhodes) between 292–280 B.C., the statue more likely stood on a promontory overlooking the harbor.

The roots of Bartholdi's idea for the Statue of Liberty were no doubt entwined with his earlier plans for a gigantic lighthouse at the entrance of the Suez Canal. He had presented his plans accompanied by a small statuette of the proposed monument to the Egyptian ruler, the Ismail Pasha in April 1869. The Egyptian ruler remarked that he preferred to see the light carried on the head of the statue, in the manner Egyptian women carried their jugs of water and other loads, rather than in a torch held by the statue's uplifted arms. Bartholdi agreed to such a modification, and left preliminary drawings with the pasha on the understanding that they would discuss the matter again several months later in Paris. Unfortunately, the colossal lighthouse was never commissioned, although the designs triggered Bartholdi's imagination and eventually led to the Statue of Liberty.

★ A SUEZ LIGHTHOUSE. In 1869, Bartholdi proposed this design for a lighthouse to be built by the Khedive of Egypt. It was to be located at the entrance of the Suez Canal; however, the project was never commissioned.

★ ÉDOUARD RENÉ DE LABOULAYE. Édouard René de Laboulaye (1811–83), a professor and leading French legal scholar, first suggested—according to Bartholdi—that a monument be built to commemorate American independence. Laboulaye organized and served as chairman of the Franco-American Union, which undertook the campaign to build the statue.

It was Laboulaye who urged his friend, Bartholdi, to undertake a trip to the United States in 1871 in hopes of encouraging a jointly sponsored monument, celebrating the longtime friendship between France and the United States. The distinguished French scholar was certain that the proposed plan would stir up enthusiasm on both sides of the Atlantic, and he wrote letters of introduction to prominent Americans for Bartholdi.

During his five months in the United States, Bartholdi did in fact meet many people. He traveled from New York to Boston, to Philadelphia, to Washington, and across the continent to Salt Lake City and San Francisco. In New York Batholdi met Horace Greeley, editor of the *New York Tribune* and in 1872 the Democratic Party's candidate for President, and George William Curtis, a powerful independent

political leader and editor of *Harper's Weekly,* two influential makers of opinion. He also talked with Peter Cooper, the civic-minded industrialist and philanthropist who had financially backed the cross-Atlantic telegraph cable to France laid by Cyrus W. Field. Bartholdi renewed his friendship with the landscape artist and writer John LaFarge, whom he had previously met in Paris. Indeed, he often stayed at the LaFarge home in Newport, Rhode Island, and it was there that he later met his future wife.

Armed with a letter of introduction, Bartholdi visited President Ulysses S. Grant at the summer White House in Long Branch, New Jersey. Grant listened carefully to Bartholdi's plan, but at no time did he ever express an interest in placing his enormous prestige behind the project.

In Philadelphia the sculptor met Colonel John W. Forney, publisher of the *Press* and a civic and political leader of considerable influence. Then early in July, Bartholdi visited the nation's capital and talked with the influential senator from Massachusetts, Charles Sumner, also a friend of Laboulaye.

On several occasions throughout the course of his 1871 trip, Bartholdi visited Boston. There he met more than once with Henry

GEN. GRANTS COTTAGE, LONG BRANCH

REMINISCENCES of GEN! GRANT,
BY
PACH BROS. 841 B. WAY.

★ ULYSSES S. GRANT. A Civil War general, Ulysses S. Grant (1822–85) was the 18th President of the United States. During the summers of his presidency (1869–77), Grant and his family resided at the popular summer resort of Long Branch, New Jersey. Here his family is shown gathered around him on the porch of his summer home.

Wadsworth Longfellow, the most popular poet of his day, at Longfellow's summer home in Nahant on a neck of land that reaches far into Massachusetts Bay. Longfellow expressed to Bartholdi his hope that the sculptor's dream of a statue in New York harbor would find interest and support among New Yorkers.

During August 1871, Bartholdi began his cross-continent tour. From Boston he traveled to Westfield, Hartford, and New Haven in Connecticut. Westward through New York, he visited Niagara Falls and passed through Canada by railroad to Detroit, and then on to Chicago. His train route took him further west to Omaha and then across the prairie to the Rocky Mountains.

The vastness of the prairie and the enormous ruggedness of the mountains fired his imagination. He stopped in Salt Lake City, where he saw the Mormon Temple and visited with Brigham Young. Bartholdi was deeply moved by his descent from the Sierra Nevadas into California and remarked: "One enters valleys and gorges, one passes through trenches and tunnels, from one ravine to the other, skirting enormous masses of rocks. Some of the sights are magnificent." He then visited San Francisco and also saw many of California's scenic wonders and landmarks.

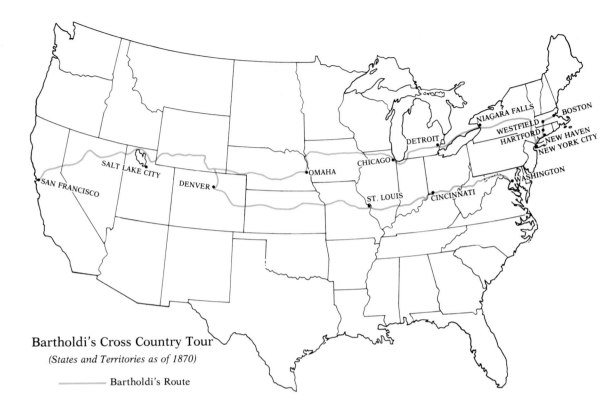

Bartholdi's Cross Country Tour
(States and Territories as of 1870)

———— Bartholdi's Route

On his way back from the west coast, Bartholdi passed through Denver and crossed the plains again. From his railroad car, he saw herds of buffalo, standing numberless against an endless horizon. Observing his traveling companions as well as Americans in general, Bartholdi thought they lacked a certain individualism, that the individual felt it necessary to agree with local opinion and swim with the stream. He felt Americans had no time to live and enjoy life. He sensed the American's desire for bigness: "Everything is big here, even the *petit pois* (green peas)." Yet, this American sense of—and desire for—grandeur gave credence to Bartholdi's hope that his monumental statue would appeal to the American people.

He stopped in St. Louis and Cincinnati, his eyes aglow in the reflection of brilliant autumn colors descending on the forests and countryside. Back in Washington for the opening of the Congress, Bartholdi hoped to enlist both public and financial support for his project. He was to be disappointed. He heard from his Washington friends that the first step for his proposed joint statue commemorating Franco-American friendship would have to be taken by the French, as the Congress of the United States was not yet ready to support the enterprise. Thwarted for the time being but undaunted, Bartholdi returned to France.

His trip to the United States had been useful, even if it had not achieved an agreement between any French and American parties to construct and erect a statue of Liberty. He had arrived in New York unknown, a man with a dream and a pocket full of letters of introduction. He had met and talked with many powerful and highly-placed Americans: from the President of the United States, to distinguished politicians, rich new industrialists, prominent literary figures, and religious leaders. With each he had spoken of his dream of a huge monument dedicated to the idea of liberty. And with each of them he had spoken of his purpose in coming to the United States in search of joint sponsorship for such a monument. Bartholdi had indeed laid a strong foundation of personal friendship with a powerful network of public figures. Notwithstanding his expertise as a sculptor of enormous monuments, Bartholdi had also displayed his considerable talents as a salesman of persuasive charm and merit.

Back in Paris

Back in his Paris studio, Bartholdi could visualize the site for his statue of liberty. While he had been in New York, he had given some attention to a proper site. A place in New York harbor was essential to Bartholdi; and a small island off the lower tip of Manhattan named Bedloe's Island seemed to provide the most attractive prospect.

For the next five years Bartholdi worked from time to time on the Statue of Liberty project, elaborating his plans and refining his designs. Originally, both he and Laboulaye had hoped that the statue would be finished by 1876, in time for the centennial celebration of the Declaration of Independence. During this same period Bartholdi accepted a commission from Adolphe Thiers, President of the French Republic, to create a monument of the Marquis de Lafayette that was to be presented to the City of New York. In the course of the Franco-Prussian War of 1870–71, the city of New York, and especially its French residents, contributed a great deal of moral and financial aid to the suffering French people. Bartholdi's statue of Lafayette was to be an expression of gratitude from the entire French nation. This work of art was unveiled to great acclaim in New York in Union Square—then the heart of New York's most fashionable business and residential area—in the centennial year of 1876.

By 1874 Laboulaye's and Bartholdi's private efforts had become formalized with the establishment of the Union Franco-Américaine Committee. The purpose of this committee was to implement the Statue of Liberty project. An appeal for funds to underwrite the expense of creating the statue was launched in French newspapers on September 28, 1875. The goal of the committee was to present the Statue of Liberty to the people of the United States on July 4, 1876, fastening anew the strong ties between the two nations.

★ LAFAYETTE. The Marquis de Lafayette's (1757–1834) steadfast courage, integrity, and idealism have made him a popular symbol of the bond between France and the United States. Located in Union Square (Park Avenue South and 15th Street) in New York City, this statue of Lafayette by Bartholdi was a gift from the French nation to the people of New York City in gratitude for support during the Franco-Prussian War (1870–71). Lafayette is shown offering his sword to the cause of American Independence.

Momentum for the project gathered in France. Two hundred guests, including descendants of the Marquis de Lafayette and the Comte de Rochambeau, gathered for a banquet on November 6, 1875, at the Grand Hotel de Louvre in Paris. Patriotic words filled the air: Recollections of the American Revolution and of Franco-American friendship issued forth. The dining hall was decorated with the flags of both republics, as well as portraits of their current presidents, Marie Edmé Patrice de MacMahon and Ulysses S. Grant. The focal point of the evening was a floodlit painting of a statue of Liberty shining at night in New York harbor, an effective visual reminder that the main purpose of the evening was to raise money for the monument. Among the speakers of the evening were Elihu B. Washburne, the American Ambassador to France, Colonel John W. Forney, the representative in Europe for the 1876 Philadelphia Centennial Exhibition, and Édouard de Laboulaye, chairman of the Union Franco-Américaine. Laboulaye spoke eloquently of the affection for Benjamin Franklin in France and for the Marquis de Lafayette in America, a theme symbolic of the occasion.

Reactions to the Statue of Liberty project as reported in the press, ranged from unbridled enthusiasm to indelicate and thoughtless criticism. One individual asked for the honor of contributing the metal for the statue; an American residing in Paris suggested that the roles should be reversed and that a statue should be erected on the banks of the Seine, and offered $10,000, a rather large sum of money for that day, to launch such a project. Indeed, in time such a project did take place and a statue—one-quarter the size of the statue in New York harbor—was built on the Île des Cygnes downstream from the Eiffel Tower.

In April 1876, a gala benefit performance took place at the Paris Opera. The renowned French musician, Charles François Gounod presented a Liberty cantata, which he had composed for the event. Once again, the now-aging Édouard de Laboulaye made a stirring speech for funds declaring:

> "This liberty will not be the one wearing a red bonnet on her head, a pike in her hand, who walks on corpses. It will be the American Liberty, who does not hold an incendiary torch but a beacon which enlightens. . . . May this statue, a monument to an old friendship, weather time and storm! One century from now America, with an enormous population, will celebrate its second Centennial. She will have forgotten us, but she will not have forgotten either Washington or Lafayette. This Statue of Liberty created in a common effort, will preserve the precious memories which are the links between the two nations; it will preserve among future generations, like a sacred tradition, the eternal friendship of the United States and France."

Later in the evening, Gounod's cantata was performed. It began with these words: "I have triumphed! I am one hundred years old! My name is Liberty!"

Ten days later, on May 6, 1876, Bartholdi left Paris with a French delegation for the United States to attend the Philadelphia Centennial Exhibition. He was to stay in America for nine months, and this visit was to prove to be the turning point in launching the Statue of Liberty.

Bartholdi's Second Visit

Arriving in Philadelphia on May 18, 1876, Bartholdi must have been particularly pleased to see his own monumental fountain placed centrally between the main exhibition building and the machinery hall. The sculptor was also eagerly anticipating the arrival of another impressive example of his artistic talents for public display: the arm from the statue holding the Torch of Liberty. However, its arrival from Paris to Philadelphia was delayed time and time again.

Nevertheless, the American press gave Bartholdi and his idea of a statue of Liberty on Bedloe's Island considerable attention. He used the pages of the newspapers and weekly magazines, as well as

the ears of any listener he could corner, to broadcast his design for the enormous statue. Traveling to New York to attend the Offenbach Supper for Artists, he sought to capture his audience with his skilled oratory, but the artists in attendance did not respond enthusiastically. Perhaps some were critical of Bartholdi's talents as a sculptor, or possibly some of them were envious because the dream of the statue was his and not theirs. Certainly they had opportunity to see the quality of the French sculptor's work, since his splendid statue of the young Marquis de Lafayette was then on display in Central Park prior to its permanent relocation to Union Square.

A few days later, on July 4, 1876, Bartholdi had the pleasure of seeing a large illuminated picture of the proposed Statue of Liberty on the side of the New York Club building in Madison Square. Several days later, the *New York Tribune* printed an enthusiastic article on "France's monumental gift to the United States." Bartholdi's name and dream were no longer unknown to Americans.

The arm of Liberty finally arrived in Philadelphia in August. The local Philadelphia newspaper, the *Press*, noted that the whole piece—the torch and part of the forearm—was thirty feet high; and with a touch of local boosterism, the paper stated that if New York did not financially support Bartholdi's dream, Philadelphia would erect the statue on George's Hill or Lemon Hill in Fairmont Park. The newspaper's statement sparked an inter-city rivalry that was to spread

International Exhibition, 1876.

2025-COLOSSAL HAND AND TORCH "LIBERTY"

★ TORCH OF LIBERTY AT PHILADELPHIA EXPOSITION. In order to raise funds, the right hand and torch of the statue were displayed in Philadelphia in 1876 at the Centennial International Exhibition, and later in New York City in Madison Square at Fifth Avenue and 23rd Street. For a fee of fifty cents, a visitor could climb the steel ladder leading to the balcony surrounding the torch. In 1884, the hand and torch were dismantled and returned to Paris for incorporation in the statue.

to many other American cities and not to be put to rest until the statue itself was finally placed on its pedestal in New York harbor.

In late August, Bartholdi, accompanied by his friend, the engineer Henri de Stucklé, traveled from New York City to Washington and made application at the U.S. Copyright Office. He registered his work and identified it as a "Statue of American Independence." Bartholdi's application was enrolled as Number 9939 of 1876; it was documented with photographs of the drawing of the Statue of Liberty and a model.

On September 6, 1876, the French sculptor was back in New York City for the unveiling in Union Square of his statue of the Marquis de Lafayette. The statue itself was a gift to the City of New York from the government of France, while the pedestal was sponsored by the French residents of New York. The ceremony was a celebration not only for Bartholdi, but also for the residents of all of New York; and the event greatly aided the campaign for the construction and erection of a statue of Liberty.

The New York Times published a curious editorial on September 29, 1876, entitled: "The French Statue." It recounted misleading and false information about the work, declaring the project had been suspended in Bartholdi's studio in Paris after $200,000 had been raised. The article reported that a substantial sum had been spent on the construction of the arm and torch now on display in Philadelphia.

★ LIBERTY LIGHTING THE WORLD'S COMMERCE. Edward Moran (1829–1901) migrated with his family from Great Britain to the United States in 1844. He was a marine painter of considerable importance. In 1871, he exhibited in Philadelphia a collection of seventy-five paintings and gave the entire profits from the exhibition to the victims of the Franco-Prussian War. His painting of the statue, sometimes known as *The Commerce of Nations Paying Homage to Liberty,* was painted in 1876 and was prominently displayed at key fund-raising events in New York City.

The editorial also, in error, declared that the Americans were now expected to pay for the rest of the statue; and if it had cost $200,000 to do an arm, then the other arm would cost a similar amount and the legs about $250,000 each. The *Times* projected that the completed and erected statue would cost about $2 million.

Bartholdi replied to *The New York Times'* editorial in a letter published on October 5th, on the pages of Colonel John W. Forney's *Press* in Philadelphia. He stated that he was acting on behalf of the Franco-Américaine Committee, which was under the chairmanship of Édouard de Laboulaye, and that it was this committee that had undertaken the task of raising funds for Liberty's construction at a cost of approximately 600,000 francs or $120,000. Further, he declared, that until he had read the *Times'* editorial, he had been certain that the distinguished list of names associated with the Statue of Liberty project—Lafayette, Rochambeau, Laboulaye, de Tocqueville, and Noailles—was sufficient to demonstrate the worthiness of the project. He was saddened that the newspaper did not understand the intention of the French committee and the artist with regard to the statue. Then with a stroke of tact and cleverness, Bartholdi added: "I now await the action of the American people, whether the work itself shall or shall not be established on Bedloe's Island by the generous cooperation of your country." Finally, Bartholdi defended himself against the charge that he would personally profit from his agreement with the Franco-Américaine Committee, pointing out that he was now visiting the United States for the second time at his own expense. Across the country newspapers joined the fray, both in support of and in opposition to the erection of the Statue of Liberty.

During the autumn of 1876, Bartholdi went briefly to Newport, Rhode Island, to visit his good friend, John LaFarge, and then on to Montreal. While in Montreal, the forty-two-year-old sculptor renewed his friendship with Jeanne-Emilie Baheux de Puysieux, a lady he had met in the LaFarge home in Newport in 1871. Then on December 20th, in the very same home of his artist friend, John LaFarge, Frédéric Auguste Bartholdi and Jeanne-Emilie Baheux de Puysieux were married.

Returning to New York on January 2, 1877, the sculptor attended a meeting of key public leaders at the Century Association. In attendance were William M. Evarts as chairman, Samuel Babcock, Richard Butler, Joseph H. Choate, Frederic R. Coudert, Judge Hilton, John Jay, Theodore Roosevelt (the father of President Theodore Roosevelt), and Henry F. Spaulding. Edward Moran's painting, "Liberty Lighting the World's Commerce," was on exhibit, and his brother, Thomas Moran, read a poem in honor of the statue. Evarts reviewed for his audience the history and purpose of the project. He stated that it was the responsibility of Americans to raise money for the construction of the foundation and pedestal on which the statue would rest. At that time the anticipated cost for the foundation and pedestal was $125,000, a sum that was to prove to be too modest. As one of the speakers that evening, Bartholdi described not only the colossal nature of the project and its transatlantic patriotic significance, but also conveyed to his listeners, his enthusiasm for the statue's erection in New York harbor. And as chairman for the evening, William M. Evarts was charged by the group to form "The American Committee on the Statue of Liberty."

Thus, Bartholdi's second visit to the United States must be acknowledged a success. The arm and torch of the Statue of Liberty appeared in Philadelphia at the Centennial Exhibition and was later moved to New York and placed at the intersection of Fifth Avenue and Broadway (Madison Square), where visitors for fifty cents could climb the ladder leading to the balcony around the torch; the artist's statue of Lafayette had been unveiled with great fanfare in New York's Union Square; and the sculptor's large fountain, which had appeared also at the Centennial Exhibition, was moved permanently from Philadelphia to Washington, where it is now located in front of the Rayburn Office Building; and finally, his marriage to Jeanne-Emilie brought a very personal sense of fulfillment.

The Committees at Work

The work of the American Committee was carefully drawn up and five subcommittees were established. Under the leadership of William M. Evarts, two committees addressed a national appeal and established contacts with Congress. A third committee supervised by Samuel Babcock fostered links with various chambers of commerce; while a fourth promoted publicity for the project. The fifth committee supervised the erection of the statue's foundation. Later on, executive and finance committees were appointed and became the key groups for completing the organization's work.

On February 22, 1877, the anniversary of the birth of George Washington, the Congress of the United States provided substantial moral support for the Statue of Liberty project by unanimously accepting the gift of the statue from France. Meanwhile a number of Americans interested in the project visited Bartholdi in his Paris studio. Such visitors included Richard Butler of the American Committee and Ulysses S. Grant, former President of the United States. During 1878 the statue's head was displayed at the Paris Universal

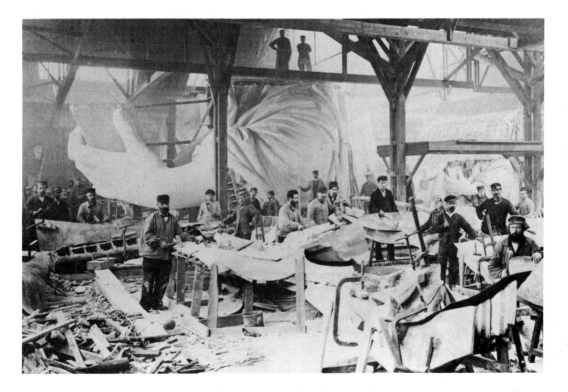

★ GAGET-GAUTHIER HAND AND ARM. The left hand and arm of the statue are seen in their early stages of construction at the workrooms of the Paris firm Gaget-Gauthier. The hand and arm are shown as full-scale model of lath and lumber; the workmen are in turn dwarfed by these models.

34

While the construction of the statue was moving along smoothly in France, the same was not true in the United States regarding the foundation and pedestal. The American press in general continued to be critical of the project; and in March 1883, Congress rejected a request for an appropriation of $100,000 to aid in the construction of the pedestal, prompting William M. Evarts to summon an emergency meeting of the American Committee to consider suspending further work on the foundation and pedestal.

News of the difficulty in raising money for the statue's final resting place triggered a response in the heart and mind of Joseph Pulitzer, publisher of *The World* in New York. A Hungarian-Jewish immigrant, Pulitzer arrived in the United States in 1864, and served in the Union Army during the Civil War. After the war he became a reporter for the St. Louis *Westliche Post,* a German-language newspaper, in 1868, and later became its managing editor and part owner. Elected to the Missouri state legislature on the Republican ticket in 1869, Pulitzer became a political figure of some importance in St. Louis politics. In 1878 he purchased both the *St. Louis Post* and the *Dispatch,* combining them as the *Post-Dispatch,* a newspaper that became a leader in Midwest journalism. In 1883 he purchased *The World* of New York from financier and stock gambler Jay Gould, and followed a policy of sensational journalism that included large headlines, feature articles, crime stories, and comic strips. Soon after purchasing *The World,* Pulitzer launched an aggressive and vigorous campaign to raise funds for the foundation and pedestal of the Statue of Liberty. The gesture was a calculated one to be sure: to raise funds for the statue; to sell newspapers for *The World;* and, for Pulitzer the Democrat, to twit the pomposity and narrow mindedness of the rich social and business establishment of New York.

A power-packed editorial kicked off Pulitzer's drive for dollars on March 14, 1883: "The Bartholdi statue will soon be on its way to New York. The great goddess comes with a torch held aloft to enlighten the world." Playing to a popular audience of people of modest means and recent immigrants, he noted that funds were necessary to build the foundation and pedestal, and that the millionaires who spend their money grandly had not come forward to do the job. The editorial concluded: "Who will save us from this national disgrace?" A few weeks later another editorial declared that: "More

GAGET-GAUTHIER FULL BODY. Through the summer and early autumn of 1883, workmen bolted copper piece to copper piece, the arm to the torso, the head to the body, and the torch to the hand. The completed statue stood 151 feet above the Rue de Chazelles.

★ JOSEPH PULITZER. Joseph Pulitzer (1847–1911), a Hungarian-Jewish immigrant, entered the United States at Castle Garden in 1864. He settled in St. Louis, where he entered the newspaper business and state politics. Pulitzer purchased the New York *World* in 1883 and quickly increased its circulation. *The World* successfully appealed for funds to complete the pedestal.

appropriate would be the gift of a statue of parsimony than a statue of liberty, if this is the appreciation we show of a friendly nation's sentiment and generosity." If the rich would not come forward with contributions for the project, what about the poor, the men and women of little wealth? The newspaper announced the establishment of a public drive to help raise funds for the pedestal, and stated that it would, in public recognition, print the names of all donors to the fund.

On May 18th Pulitzer's paper printed an extract from the Cincinnati *Commercial Gazette* proclaiming that if a Midwestern city such as St. Louis, Cincinnati, or Chicago had only to furnish a pedestal, the task would be quickly accomplished. To be sure there was an element of inter-city boosterism at play. Three days later, *The World* suggested to its readers a national campaign for funds, since "the whole country should feel interested in providing a pedestal for the Bartholdi statue." Notwithstanding these journalistic pleas, only a trickle of money came into the offices of the newspaper, and by mid-May only $135.75 had been raised!

The World published on its pages suggestions by its readers regarding methods for raising money. Thomas Foley, Alderman of the City of New York, felt the city should contribute a portion of the funds needed to construct the pedestal, while a tavernkeeper felt that the state should donate the funds, and still other writers thought the federal government should meet the burden. By June, the campaign by *The World* to raise funds for the statue fizzled out: perhaps the circulation of the newspaper was still too small; perhaps the American public was just not ready to do more.

The American Committee continued to attempt to raise money but also with relatively little success. On November 12, 1883, the chief engineer of the pedestal project, Major General Charles P. Stone, a veteran of the Mexican and Civil wars, indicated that it would cost another $148,000 to complete the construction of the pedestal, or nearly double the amount that had already been raised.

Meanwhile in France, one of the original prime movers of the Liberty project, Édouard de Laboulaye, died. He was succeeded as chairman of the French Committee by Ferdinand de Lesseps, builder of the Suez Canal; and on July 4, 1884, the official presentation of the Statue of Liberty took place. Levi P. Morton, the American Minister to France, was in attendance and the statue was outfitted with French and American banners. About two hundred people were present, including many Americans who lived in Paris. The French premier, Jules Ferry, was ill and unable to attend. Ferdinand de Lesseps presided and announced to the audience that the French government had agreed to underwrite the cost of transportation to move the statue to the United States. He also thanked Auguste Bartholdi and his associates at the firm of Gaget-Gauthier for their efforts in the design and construction of the statue. Then turning to the American Minister to France, Levi P. Morton, he continued:

> This work, Mr. Minister, is the product of enthusiasm, of devotion, of intelligence, and of the noblest sentiment which can animate man. It is great in its conception and in its realization. It is colossal in its proportions, and we hope that it will grow still larger through its moral value, thanks to the remembrances and the sentiments which it is to perpetuate. We commit it to your care, Mr. Minister, that it may remain forever the pledge of bonds which shall unite France and the great American nation.

Mr. Morton replied by reading a telegram from the President of the United States, Chester A. Arthur. He too acknowledged the outstanding efforts of the sculptor and his coworkers, and thanked the people of France for their testimony of friendship. During the ceremony a band played the national anthems of France and the United States, and following the formalities refreshments were served at the offices of Gaget-Gauthier. Still later a luncheon was held in honor of Mr. Morton and the day's activities were brought to a close with a reception at the United States legation.

The original plan was to dismantle the statue after the ceremonies, crate the parts, and then ship them to the United States. However, since the foundation and pedestal for the statue on Bedloe's Island were still incomplete, the statue remained in Paris on display for the public. One famous visitor was Victor Hugo, the author. On seeing the statue he remarked, "It is superb!" After climbing the stairs inside the statue, and before leaving, Hugo said with words that must have rung in Bartholdi's ears: "Yes, this beautiful work aims at what I have always loved and called for: peace between America and France— France which is Europe—this pledge of peace will be permanent. It was a good thing that this should have been done."

The statue was closed to the public in January 1885, and the work of disassembling it was begun. The workers numbered each part and section of the statue before crating them carefully. Now the task at hand was to complete the American side of the project.

Fund-raising efforts continued to move slowly in the United States. Between December 1, 1884, and March 10, 1885, a mere $15,662.19 came in. The treasurer of the American Committee reported

★ CORNERSTONE CEREMONY. On August 5, 1884, one month after the gift of the statue from the people of France to the people of the United States, the cornerstone of the pedestal was laid on Bedloe's Island in rain-drenched ceremonies.

38

that $182,491.40 had been donated and $179,624.51 had been spent. The Committee's fund consisted of only $2,866.89, not enough to meet the current bills for the construction of the pedestal. The project was now at a critical turning point: Should construction of the pedestal proceed on the basis that funds would hopefully be received? Neither Congress, the state of New York, or the New York City government had come forward with financial assistance, and the energetic campaign of Joseph Pulitzer and *The World* had not been successful.

During 1884, construction on the pedestal had proceeded under the supervision of the chief engineer, Major General Charles P. Stone, and the chief architect, Richard Morris Hunt. At two o'clock on the rain-soaked afternoon of August 5, 1884, the cornerstone of the pedestal was laid before an audience of fifteen hundred Americans and Frenchmen. The cornerstone, a large six-ton block of granite, came from a quarry in Leete, Connecticut. A copper box filled with a variety of items was enclosed in the cornerstone. Among the items were: a fifty-cent coin minted in 1824, the year the Marquis de Lafayette visited the United States; a coin inscribed with the words of one General Dix, "If any man attempts to haul down the American flag shoot him on the spot"; and the calling cards of the dignitaries present at the ceremony. The leaders of the American Committee earnestly hoped that the laying of the pedestal's cornerstone would encourage a new wave of contributions toward its construction. However, that was not to be. In a few weeks, all building ceased because of a lack of funds.

The situation looked quite hopeless in the early spring of 1885. New York newspapers continued to undermine the project with critical articles ridiculing the statue. Their theme was simple: The *French* should pay for the pedestal for *their statue*. With such sentiments circulated widely in print, it was no wonder that contributions dwindled to nothing. Cities such as Boston, Cleveland, and San Francisco now joined Philadelphia in offering a home to the statue; and each city, with no small sense of civic pride, declared that they could raise the money now!

The American Committee estimated that $100,000 was needed to finish the job. William M. Evarts, Richard Butler, and Henry F. Spaulding issued a stirring appeal to the public for funds stating: "If the money is not forthcoming, the statue must return to its donors, to the everlasting disgrace of the American people, or it must go to some other city, to the everlasting disgrace of New York. Citizens of the state, citizens of the metropolis, we ask you once and for all to prevent so painful and humiliating a catastrophe!"

Pulitzer to the Rescue

Undaunted by the failure of *The World*'s 1883 campaign for funds for construction of the pedestal, Joseph Pulitzer launched a new effort on March 16, 1885. His New York newspaper was in a stronger position now: In two years the circulation had risen from a few thousand to more than one hundred thousand copies a day. *The World* had successfully championed the presidential candidacy of Grover Cleveland on the Democratic ticket in 1884: Pulitzer's newspaper now carried real political clout.

Pulitzer penned stirring words to initiate the new public fund drive for construction of the pedestal:

> Money must be raised to complete the pedestal for the Bartholdi Statue. It would be an irrevocable disgrace to New York City and the American Republic to have France send this splendid gift without our having provided even so much as a landing place for it . . . The statue is now completed and ready to be brought to our shores in a vessel especially commissioned for the purpose by the French Government. Congress, by a refusal to appropriate the necessary money to complete preparations for its proper reception and erection, has thrown the responsibility back to the American people. There is but one thing that can be done, *We must raise the money! The World* is the people's paper, and it now appeals to the people to come forward and raise this money. The $250,000 that the making of the statue cost was paid in by the masses of the French people by the workingmen, the tradesmen, the shop girls, the artisans—by all, irrespective of class or condition. Let us respond in like manner. Let us not wait for the millionaires to give this money. It is not a gift from the millionaires of France to the millionaires of America, but a gift of the whole people of France to the whole people of America. Take this appeal to yourself personally. *It is meant for every reader of The World.* Give something, however little. Send it to us. We will receive it, and see that it is properly applied. We will also publish the name of every giver, however small the sum given. Let us hear from the people.

Day after day, week-in and week-out, for five months *The World* persistently urged its readers to give money for the pedestal. The day after the beginning of the fund drive, the newspaper started publishing the names of donors and the amounts given. Among the first donors was the Ten-o'clock Poker Club, which gave the contents of its first jackpot of the day—four dollars. Gifts from individuals were usually more modest and frequently accompanied with a brief letter: "I am a young man of foreign birth and have seen enough of monarchical governments to appreciate the blessings of this republic. Inclosed please find $2.00 for the Bartholdi Fund"—*Nathan Fleisch*, Orange, N.J., March 17. From another reader, "I have already given my 'mite' (through our G.A.R. post) towards the Bartholdi pedestal Fund, but inclose a little more—$1.00. Every American ought to take pride in aiding this enterprise, and it is a shame that the work of providing a place for the noble gift has, for lack of funds, been delayed so long"—*Oliver C. Cooper*, Ovid, Seneca County, N.Y., March 25.

Pulitzer carefully planned a competitive campaign for donations to the pedestal fund. The newspaper claimed that as "[Grover] Cleveland was elected . . . the pedestal will be erected." *The World* established a prize of two double-eagle coins (about $40 in gold) to the donor who contributed the most money. It urged its readers to give twenty-five cents to the campaign and to encourage their friends to do so too. The other New York newspapers, despite an invitation from Pulitzer, remained aloof from the drive for funds: The campaign for a pedestal for Bartholdi's statue was *The World*'s project.

An element of class conflict and rivalry hovered in the background of the campaign, occasionally breaking into the open: Rich established figures in the community, such as Jay Gould and William H. Vanderbilt, appeared to react against recent immigrants like Joseph

★ JAY GOULD. A New York speculator and financier, Jay Gould (1836–92) and his group controlled the Erie Railroad. He once attempted to corner the gold market. *(Left)*

★ WILLIAM HENRY VANDERBILT. Son of "Commodore" Cornelius Vanderbilt, William Henry Vanderbilt (1821–85) succeeded his father as president of The New York Central Railroad and doubled the $100 million fortune that he inherited. *(Right)*

Pulitzer. Certainly the business and financial community had not stepped forward in an encouraging way to promote and assist the erection of the statue on Bedloe's Island. To taunt the reluctant business and social leaders of New York, *The World* stated in its March 19, 1885, issue that William H. Vanderbilt and Jay Gould had contributed a five-hundred dollar *Confederate note* to the fund drive—in other words, a gift that was worthless. On another occasion *The World* published a letter from a contributor that chided the rich and mighty: "A few poor fellows whose pockets are not as deep as a well, but whose love for Liberty is wider than a church door, hand you the enclosed $7.25 of their might towards the Bartholdi pedestal fund. May heaven help you in your good work; it seems that New York's rich men do not."

Children as well as adults joined the campaign. A letter from Florence DeForrest of Metuchen, New Jersey, declared: "I am a little girl, nine years old, and would like to do something for the Statue Fund. I will send you a pair of my pet-game bantams if you will sell them and give the money to the Statue." *The World* informed its readers of the well-being of the birds at the newspaper office on a daily basis . . . selling the birds several times over until the success of the campaign prompted *The World* to return the bantams. Still another youngster wrote: "Please take this from a little boy who wants to set Jay Gould a good example. I read *The World* every day and am ten years old. Inclosed find ten cents, my pocket piece"—*Young Patriot*.

By March 27th 2,535 persons had contributed $2,359.67 for the pedestal fund. *The World* contributed another $1,000. The goal of raising $100,000 was a long way off, particularly when the campaign was for pennies, nickels, and dimes from many people rather than $100, $500, or $1,000 gifts from a few. Each day the list of contributors printed by the newspaper grew longer, and each day the New York public looked forward to reading about the progress of the fund drive.

On April 1st the newspaper announced that the crated parts of the Statue of Liberty would leave France on May 8th. Two weeks later, an editorial in *The World* appealed to William H. Vanderbilt to contribute his hourly income, said to amount to $1,250. A day later Jay Gould, who it was said received an hourly income of $500, received the newspaper's spotlight. Perhaps the editorial strategy was to provide the reader with pointed, comic relief. And it worked: It stimulated additional interest and donations to the fund.

All around New York contribution boxes were placed in bars and public places. A number of organizations undertook to offer programs, the proceeds of which would go to the construction of the pedestal. The Eden Musée presented a display of figures of the Presidents of the United States, surrounding a replica of the Statue of Liberty; while the Columbia Maenner Choir, a German singing ensemble, offered a concert at Steinway Hall.

Money flowed into the fund in small amounts, and still more names were added to the daily list of donors. From Newark, New Jersey, came a note: "I see by the paper this morning, that a little boy, one year old, contributed one dollar to the pedestal fund. Although I cannot creep, I can shout for the cause of liberty when my papa and mama want to sleep. Enclose please find one dollar from a little boy eight months"—*Sumner D. Aspenwald, Jr.* By April 15th just over $25,000 had been raised, and one month later another $25,000. Now half the $100,000 needed to complete the pedestal was in hand. The American Committee gave orders for work to proceed again.

The Goal Is in Sight

On the other side of the Atlantic the operations for moving the Statue of Liberty from Paris to New York began. Seventeen railroad cars carried the crated statue from Paris to Rouen, an inland port on the Seine River. The crates were hoisted aboard the *Isère*, which sailed from Rouen on May 21st, arriving in New York on June 17th. Just outside the harbor, the French North Atlantic Naval Squadron met the ship and escorted it proudly into port, colors flying in full regalia. Commandant de Saune of the *Isère* presented the statue to General Stone, the chief engineer. The document of transfer had been signed by the President of the French Republic and by other public officials, as well as by Auguste Bartholdi. The City of New York gave the officers and crew of the *Isère* a rousing public greeting, including a parade through the city and an official welcome at City Hall. On July 22nd the crates began to be unloaded near the still-uncompleted pedestal on Bedloe's Island.

The arrival of the crated Statue of Liberty impelled *The World* to redouble its efforts for contributions. On June 19th the $75,000 mark was passed on the way to the $100,000 goal. Finally, on August 11, 1885, *The World*'s banner headline triumphantly read: ONE HUNDRED THOUSAND DOLLARS! TRIUMPHANT COMPLETION OF *THE WORLD*'S FUND FOR THE LIBERTY PEDESTAL. One hundred and twenty thousand persons had donated $102,000 for the erection of the pedestal. The round of fund raising finished, Joseph Pulitzer's popular effort was widely recognized as a resounding success. Young

The Copies of THE WORLD Printed and
Sold on Sunday Last Aggregated

230,220.

The Average Circulation of THE SUNDAY WORLD
is Larger than that of any other Newspaper Published
on the Western Hemisphere.

The World.

The Copies of THE WORLD Printed and
Sold on Sunday Last Aggregated

230,220.

The Average Circulation of THE SUNDAY WORLD
is Larger than that of any other Newspaper Published
on the Western Hemisphere.

VOL. XXVI., NO. 8,757.   NEW YORK, TUESDAY, AUGUST 11, 1885---WITH SUPPLEMENT.   PRICE TWO CENTS.

THE SPECTRE IN GRANADA.

A CONDITION MORE HORRIBLE THAN THAT OF NAPLES LAST YEAR.

Cholera Victims Decaying in the Streets—Three Hundred Deaths in Marseilles—Missionaries Massacred by Black Flags in Tonquin—Fatal Fall of an English Railway Station Roof.

MADRID, Aug. 10.—Granada is to-day in a most desperate condition, as a result of the ravages of cholera. The state of affairs there is really worse than it was in Naples last year during the cholera epidemic in that city. There are no doctors now in Granada, and the dead bodies of cholera victims lie unburied in the streets. There were 4,311 new cases of cholera and 1,511 deaths from the disease reported yesterday throughout all Spain.

PALERMO, Aug. 10.—A largely attended public meeting was held here last evening for the purpose of taking action to prevent the introduction of cholera. A resolution was adopted recommending that petitions be forwarded immediately to the Government, asking that complete isolation be granted to Sicily.

PARIS, Aug. 10.—Reports from Marseilles received to-day state that the weather is again very warm, and that the cholera is increasing to such an extent that the hospitals have been packed for the reception of patients suffering from the disease. Reports from Toulon state that two deaths from cholera have occurred here, and that several new cases are reported.

TOULON, Aug. 10.—The sanitary condition of this city is excellent, and it is not believed that cholera will prevail.

GIBRALTAR, Aug. 10.—No person having died here to-day apparently from cholera, the Spanish authorities promptly instituted a land cordon, barring Gibraltar from communication with the contiguous Spanish territory. This action is proving a source of much annoyance to many persons in Gibraltar, whose families reside in adjacent villages which they cannot reach under the new arrangement.

MARSEILLES, Aug. 10.—There were 300 deaths from cholera in this city during the past week.

WASHINGTON, Aug. 10.—The State Department is informed of one case of cholera at Malaga and four at Gibraltar.

THE FUNERAL AS VIEWED IN LONDON.

Spontaneous Outpouring of People Without a Parallel in History.

LONDON, Aug. 10.—All the morning newspapers to-day publish copious accounts of the funeral of Gen. Grant. All agree that the outpouring of the people on the occasion and the deep grief as indicated by the despatches were something wonderful. The Times has a special despatch three columns long detailing the scenes and incidents of the funeral and also prints a leading editorial praising and recalling many personal traits of the dead General.

MURDERED IN HIS HOME.

A WEALTHY BROOKLYNITE SHOT DOWN BY A HIDDEN FOE.

Albert R. Herrick, Whose Place of Business is at No. 60 William Street, this City, Dies Before He Can Tell Who Fired the Fatal Shot—The Police Without a Clue.

At 1.30 o'clock Mr. Albert R. Herrick, who has his place of business at the corner of Myrtle avenue and Pearl street, was promenading in front of that store with a sick child when Mr. Herrick passed to his house, which is next door, on his way from business. He bade her a pleasant "good afternoon," and then entered by the front door. Mrs. Franck started towards Johnson street, but before she had gone far she turned to retrace her steps. As she passed the Herrick residence she heard a noise as if somebody was endeavoring to force open the basement door, which is immediately under the front stoop. Mrs. Franck hurried towards the area gate, when she was startled by a pistol-shot. A second later Mr. Herrick staggered up the steps, with blood gushing from his mouth.

"Oh! what is the matter, Mr. Herrick?" cried the affrighted woman.

"Murder! Burglars! Police!" screamed Mr. Herrick.

Then he grasped his left breast, reeled and fell backward, striking the back of his head upon the coping-stone. Physicians were at once summoned but he was dead.

ONE HUNDRED THOUSAND DOLLARS!

TRIUMPHANT COMPLETION OF THE WORLD'S FUND FOR THE LIBERTY PEDESTAL.

Story of the Greatest Popular Subscription Ever Raised in America—How the Republic Was Saved from Lasting Disgrace—An Event for Patriotic Citizens to Rejoice Over—A Roll of Honor Bearing the Names of 120,000 Generous Patriots—The Flags of France and the American Union Floating in Sisterly Sympathy—Over $2,300 Received Yesterday—The Grand Total Foots Up $102,006.39—A Generous Lady Pays $130 for the Washington Cent.

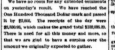

THIS PEDESTAL TO LIBERTY WAS PROVIDED BY THE VOLUNTARY CONTRIBUTIONS OF 120,000 PATRIOTIC CITIZENS OF THE AMERICAN UNION THROUGH THE NEW YORK WORLD FINIS CORONAT OPUS

We have no room for any extended comments on yesterday's result. We have reached the One Hundred Thousand Dollar mark and passed it by $2,000. The receipts of the day were $2,300.93, which makes the grand total $102,006.39. There is need for all this money and more, so that we are glad to have a surplus over the amount we originally expected to gather.

people and old people, school children and laborers, members of Grand Army of the Republic posts near and far . . . all had contributed to the fund to complete the pedestal. So too had the employees of many business firms: More than twelve hundred and fifty staff members of the American Express Company in offices across the country had donated to the fund. Employees of the Bank of New York, McKesson & Robbins, and the Knickerbocker Ice Company were well represented among the contributors.

To commemorate the completion of the fund drive, *The World* ran a poem which declared:

> Ah, Madame Liberty, God bless you!
> Since all the cash is here at hand,
> No longer need it now to stress you
> The question of a place to stand . . .
>
> Soon in your allotted station
> Firm in your tower strong and tall,
> Will give this truth a new illustration,
> THE PEOPLE ARE THE ALL AND ALL.

Work on the pedestal continued for another eight months before Bartholdi could assist Chief Engineer Stone in planning the final steps for mounting the statue. Arriving on November 4, 1885, aboard the transatlantic steamer *Amérique*, Bartholdi immediately entered a round of social events: dinner at Joseph Pulitzer's mansion at 616 Fifth Avenue; a dinner at the Union League Club, hosted by the American Committee in Bartholdi's honor; and dinner with former President Chester A. Arthur. His work finished, Bartholdi set sail back to France aboard the *Normandie* on November 25th.

★ FRONT PAGE OF THE NEW YORK *WORLD*. The front page of Joseph Pulitzer's New York *World* chronicled the five-month campaign in 1885 to solicit funds for the completion of the pedestal for the Statue of Liberty. Pulitzer's persistent efforts not only raised the necessary funds, but also increased his newspaper's circulation until it became the largest in the Western Hemisphere.

★ DESIGN DRAWING OF PEDESTAL. The Paris-educated American architect, Richard Morris Hunt (1828–95), designed the massive pedestal. The final design was completed in August 1884; it fully complemented—without rivaling—the majesty of the statue itself.

★ PEDESTAL IN PROGRESS. At the time of its construction, Liberty's pedestal was the largest single concrete mass ever built. The foundation is 52 feet 10 inches high. At the bottom it is 91 feet square, while at the top it is 65 feet square.

PLAN AT A

PLAN AT B

The pedestal was finally completed in April 1886, and work began at once to mount the statue, a task that was to take six months. First, the massive iron framework designed by the brilliant French engineer, Gustave Eiffel, to withstand the strongest gusts in a very windy harbor, was anchored to the pedestal. Then, the plate sections of the statue itself were uncrated one by one and carefully attached in place to the towering frame. The unveiling date was set for October 28, 1886.

On October 25th a French delegation that included Bartholdi, his wife, and Ferdinand de Lesseps, Chairman of the French Committee, arrived aboard the liner *La Bretagne*. Greeted by the American Committee and Joseph Pulitzer, they all boarded the yacht *Atillie* and sailed toward Bedloe's Island to view the Statue of Liberty. Surrounded by newspaper reporters eager to record his words, Bartholdi did not disappoint them. *The World* reported his statement: "The dream of my life is accomplished . . . I see the symbol of unity and friendship between two nations—two great republics, . . ." and speaking to de Lesseps he commented, "It's a consolation to know that this statue will exist thousands of years from now, long after our names shall have been forgotten."

De Lesseps in his turn declared: "It has surpassed my expectations. I was prepared for a great work of art, but this is sublime. It is simply faultless." Another member of the French delegation, General Pelletier, noted: "Indeed, Liberty Island was created for Bartholdi's statue, not the statue for the island!"

Bartholdi and the French delegation made the Hoffman House, an exclusive hotel at Broadway between 24th and 25th Streets, their headquarters during their stay in the city. After much private wining and dining, the American Committee officially welcomed the French delegation at a reception held on October 26th at the Academy of Music. The next day at City Hall, Mayor William R. Grace presented Bartholdi with the Freedom of the City, and that evening the French party and New York's civic and social leaders attended a splendid reception at the Union League Club. Among the guests were William

★ DESIGN DRAWING OF ARMATURE AND PEDESTAL: ALEXANDRE GUSTAVE EIFFEL. The noted French engineer, Alexandre Gustave Eiffel (1832–1923), was a builder of bridges, viaducts, and the designer of the Eiffel Tower for the 1889 World Exhibition. His design for the framework of the statue is shown set on top of Richard Morris Hunt's pedestal. Concrete, stone, iron, and copper each locked to one another, combining the genius of Hunt, Eiffel, and Bartholdi.

50

★ GROVER CLEVELAND. Grover Cleveland (1837–1908) served as the 22nd and 24th President of the United States. He championed civil service reform.

M. Evarts, John Pierpont Morgan, Theodore Roosevelt (the father of President Theodore Roosevelt), Elihu Root, and many other distinguished people. Once more a painting of Liberty by Edward Moran commanded full attention at the reception.

Unveiling day—October 28, 1886—was filled with celebration. Despite rain, tens of thousands jammed the four-mile parade route, which started at Fifth Avenue and 57th Street, moved southward and where the paving was incomplete, the route detoured down Madison Avenue, and then down Broadway to the Battery. French and American flags flew everywhere. Public offices were closed, and Mayor Grace issued a proclamation urging shopkeepers to close during the hours of the parade. The parade route passed a presidential reviewing stand at Madison Square Park, where Grover Cleveland, some of his Cabinet members, Bartholdi, and de Lesseps reviewed the 20,000 marchers. The strains of the French and United States national anthems repeatedly filled the air, played by one marching band after another. Among the marchers were veterans groups, public officials, judges, and governors, French-speaking societies in New York, and college students from Columbia and City College. Policemen and firemen from nearby and distant cities, such as Philadelphia and Baltimore, also joined the line of march.

★ INAUGURATION DAY PARADE BY LAND. A million people, waving the Stars and Stripes of the United States and the Tricolor of France, lined the five-mile parade route down Fifth Avenue on October 28, 1886. Twenty thousand rain-soaked marchers paraded from 57th Street to the Battery.

★ THE UNVEILING OF THE STATUE OF LIBERTY. The refinement and drama of Edward Moran's 1886 painting, *The Unveiling of the Statue of Liberty (right)*, is in contrast to his painting of the statue ten years earlier *(above)*. The proposed pedestal of 1876 lacked the form and grandeur of Richard Morris Hunt's later design. The statue's dedication is heralded by the smoking cannons of Fort Wood, bandsmen on barges, and the brilliant colors of the American Stars and Stripes and the French Tricolor.

The last unit passed the reviewing stand soon after 1 o'clock that afternoon. President Cleveland and his party then went to the 23rd Street pier, where they embarked on a yacht to Bedloe's Island. Meanwhile, the parade ended at the Battery at the foot of Manhattan Island across the harbor from Bedloe's Island.

At 12:45 P.M. a nautical parade began: Some three hundred ships moved slowly down the rainy and foggy Hudson River from the area of the 42nd Street pier. They were heading to form a crescent in the harbor below Bedloe's Island. The plan was to have the ships blow their whistles, sound their sirens, and fire their guns at the moment the flag of France covering Liberty's face dropped away.

President Cleveland reached Bedloe's Island at 3 o'clock to the strains of band music and proceeded to the speakers' platform, which was decorated with a large banner on which was painted in large letters: A. BARTHOLDI AND LIBERTY. Master of Ceremonies

★ FIREWORKS FOLLOWING INAUGURATION. Poor weather conditions delayed the inaugural fireworks display for three nights. Finally on November 1, 1886, with tugboats and steamers encircling Bedloe's Island, a display of rockets, shooting-stars, and bombs was launched, brilliantly illuminating the harbor with cascading red, white, and blue sparks. At seven o'clock, a bright white light radiated through the lenses of the statue's torch—the torch was lit.

General Scholfield opened the ceremony; the Reverend Richard S. Storrs, a minister from Brooklyn, gave the invocation. Speaking on behalf of the Union Franco-Américaine, of which he was president, Ferdinand de Lesseps then addressed the throng. He was followed by William M. Evarts, Chairman of the American Committee, immediately after which the unveiling of the statue was to take place. Meanwhile Bartholdi had taken his place inside the statue's crown. He was to pull the rope that removed the flag covering the face of the statue. During a pause in Evart's speech, the French flag was removed and the statue's face appeared. The speaker was forgotten: Pandemonium ensued. The people cheered. Ships in the harbor sounded their horns and whistles, while their guns saluted the Statue of Liberty.

President Cleveland arose to address the audience after the noise had diminished, and in his clear and powerful voice proclaimed:

We will not forget that Liberty has made here her home, nor shall her chosen altar be neglected. Willing voteries will constantly keep alive its fires and these shall gleam upon the shores of our sister republic in the east. Reflected thence and joined with answering rays, a stream of light shall pierce the darkness of ignorance and man's oppression until Liberty enlightens the world.

Cleveland was followed by the Minister Plenipotentiary and Delegate Extraordinary of the French government, who, speaking in English, paid eloquent tribute for the generations to come of the statue's symbolic hope: "Among the thousands of Europeans who are daily conveyed to these hospitable shores, no one will pass before this glorious emblem without immediately perceiving its moral greatness and without greeting it with respect and thankfulness."

Following a long address by the Honorable Chauncey M. Depew and the singing of the doxology, "Praise God from whom all blessings flow," the benediction was delivered by the Episcopal Bishop of New York, the Right Reverend Henry C. Potter, and the throngs went on to their private celebrations and memories of the day. A new symbol and an old tradition were now firmly rooted in the bedrock of New York harbor, gateway to America.

★ BARTHOLDI'S WATERCOLOR OF THE STATUE. In addition to his work as a sculptor, Bartholdi enjoyed a life-long interest in painting. This watercolor of the statue was painted in 1888 for an old family friend, Mrs. Rosetta Laubheim Lumley of New York and Paris.

★ STATUE OF LIBERTY, ABOUT 1886. Soon after the dedication of the statue on October 28, 1886, this souvenir view of the Statue of Liberty and of Bartholdi was printed. Celebrating the gift of the people of France to the people of the United States, this souvenir depicts the majestic and monumental form of Liberty rising above the cannons and walls of Fort Wood.

The First Hundred Years

At the time of its dedication, the Statue of Liberty was the tallest structure in New York City. Reaching to a height of 305 feet, her torch sparkled above such "skyscraping" neighbors as the Western Union Telegraph Building (230 feet), the Trinity Church steeple (286 feet), the Tribune Building (282 feet), and the Brooklyn Bridge towers (282 feet). Not until 1899, the eve of the twentieth century, was she overtaken by St. Paul's Building, which rose to 310 feet; and during each decade since, new buildings rose higher and higher until the twin towers of the World Trade Center soared to an astonishing 1,377 feet. Yet our lady of the harbor dramatically holds her own as the visual and inspirational center of the harbor skyline.

From 1886 to 1902, the Lighthouse Board, an agency of the federal government, administered and maintained the Statue of Liberty. This arrangement was required by the terms of an 1877 resolution by Congress that the statue was to be maintained as a *lighthouse*. Having designed the statue before the advent of electric

★ NEW YORK HARBOR, ABOUT 1892. The view of New York harbor changed considerably between 1871 and 1892. The most noticeable change, as can be seen in this Currier and Ives print of 1892, was the inspiring presence of Bartholdi's Statue of Liberty on Bedloe's Island.

lights, Bartholdi's plans called for kerosene light to radiate out from the diadem, while an observation platform surrounded the torch. However, just one month before the dedication ceremonies, the torch was electrified. Notwithstanding the symbolic role of *Liberty Enlightening the World* (the statue's original name) as a beacon for ships and mariners, the torch's "flame," in fact, serves no practical purpose.

One day in 1903, workmen fastened a bronze tablet to an interior wall of the pedestal. No ceremony or speech marked the event, as had taken place at the laying of the cornerstone and the dedication of the statue. No New York newspaper even reported the event. Cast as part of the plaque was a poem, a poem written twenty years earlier by Emma Lazarus. She had been asked to write a poem in 1883 to aid the campaign to raise funds for the pedestal. A genteel lady of New York society and a Sephardic Jew, she was deeply affected by the spirit that inspired the creation of the statue. She was equally distressed by the massacres of Jews then taking place in Russia: a tyrannic excess that led to a mass exodus of Jews from that country. Her words voiced a universal protest against political and religious bondage:

> Not like the brazen giant of Greek fame,
> With conquering limbs astride from land to land;
> Here at our sea-washed, sunset gates shall stand
> A mighty woman with a torch, whose flame
> Is the imprisoned lightning, and her name
> Mother of Exiles. From her beacon hand
> Glows world-wide welcome; her mild eyes command
> The air-bridged harbor that twin cities frame.
> "Keep, ancient lands, your storied pomp!" cries she
> With silent lips. "Give me your tired, your poor,
> Your huddled masses yearning to breathe free,
> The wretched refuse of your teeming shore,
> Send these, the homeless, tempest-tost to me,
> I lift my lamp beside the golden door!"

In 1916 *The World* appealed to its readers on behalf of the beloved statue: This time *The World* sought funds to modernize the statue and to enhance her nighttime appearance. And once again the public opened its heart and purse, contributing $30,000 to floodlight the statue at night. The torch was also redesigned in glass. The Statue of Liberty now took on that dramatic radiance in the darkness for which she is so well known. In a ceremony aboard the presidential yacht on December 2, 1916, President Woodrow Wilson, accompanied by the French ambassador to the United States, Jules Jusserand, dedicated

★ EMMA LAZARUS'S *NEW COLOSSUS.* Emma Lazarus (1849–87), a New York-born poet, spoke with passion on behalf of her fellow Jews during the Russian pogroms of the 1880s. Asked by friends to write a poem to assist the struggling campaign to raise funds to build the statue, her sonnet, *The New Colossus,* seen here in her own hand, became the credo for thousands of new immigrants.

> The New Colossus.
>
> Not like the brazen giant of Greek fame,
> With conquering limbs astride from land to land;
> Here at our sea-washed, sunset gates shall stand
> A mighty woman with a torch, whose flame
> Is the imprisoned lightning, and her name
> Mother of Exiles. From her beacon-hand
> Glows world-wide welcome, her mild eyes command
> The air-bridged harbor that twin-cities frame.
>
> "Keep, ancient lands, your storied pomp!" cries she
> With silent lips. "Give me your tired, your poor,
> Your huddled masses yearning to breathe free,
> The wretched refuse of your teeming shore,
> Send these, the homeless, tempest-tost to me,
> I lift my lamp beside the golden door!"
>
> Emma Lazarus.
>
> November 2nd 1883.

the new lighting system. In his address, Wilson remarked: "There has come more and more into my heart the conviction that peace is going to come to the world only with liberty." His words were spoken against the dark background of a world divided and a Europe torn by war.

During World War I, the Statue of Liberty became a new national symbol, replacing *Columbia*, the female figure that had been a popular representation of America since the Revolutionary War. Liberty's features now appeared everywhere in the country, on millions of posters encouraging Americans to buy war bonds to finance the U.S. war effort. There were four "Liberty loan drives" during 1917 and 1918 that featured the statue, and they were impressive successes. The U.S. government sold about $15 billion worth of bonds, equal to about half the cost of the war! The posters showed Liberty in a variety of poses: Sometimes the statue was removed from its pedestal and became the female counterpart to Uncle Sam; on some posters, Liberty was draped in the stars and stripes, while in others she was represented as a warrior.

Responsibility for the administration and maintenance of the statue passed from the Lighthouse Board to the War Department in 1902. This change was quite natural, since most of Bedloe's Island was then a U.S. Army installation, Fort Wood. Indeed, even after the National Park Service assumed responsibility for maintaining the statue in 1933, the Army continued to control most of the island, with warehouses, barracks, and other buildings cluttering the island.

60

★ LIBERTY BOND POSTERS. Not until the outbreak of World War I did the Statue of Liberty become a national and international symbol of freedom and peace. To help finance U.S. participation in the war, the Treasury Department authorized five bond issues. The first four were called Liberty loans and in their highly successful advertising campaigns used the Statue of Liberty as a rallying symbol.

On October 28, 1936, about twelve years after President Calvin Coolidge had declared the Statue of Liberty a national monument, President Franklin Delano Roosevelt traveled to Bedloe's Island to commemorate the statue's fiftieth birthday. Dark clouds covered the United States and Europe. The effects of the Great Depression could be seen everywhere across the nation: Factories closed; farms were foreclosed; the unemployed sold apples and pencils on street corners and knocked on doors for food. In Europe Benito Mussolini and Adolph Hitler charted ominous courses for their nations that deeply unsettled the leaders of the world's democracies. October 28 was a beautiful autumn day. The President was surrounded by civic leaders, diplomats, soldiers, and boy scouts. Although there were fewer persons on the island for these ceremonies than had been present fifty years earlier at the unveiling, President Roosevelt's words were heard by millions over radio. Even though he was in the final days of his first re-election campaign, the President did not speak of politics. Nor did he spend many words on the statue itself. He reminded his vast audience that:

> Fifty years ago our old neighbor and friend from across the sea gave us this monument to stand at the principal eastern gateway to the New World. Grover Cleveland, President of the United States, accepted this gift with the pledge that "we will not forget that liberty has here made her home; nor shall her chosen altar be neglected."
>
> During those fifty years that covenant between ourselves and our most cherished convictions has not been broken. . . .

President Roosevelt spoke of America as the home of liberty, the vision of America as the land of promise. For more than three centuries, streams of men, women, and children followed the beacon of liberty that since 1886 the statue's torch had come to symbolize. They came to America for freedom of worship, freedom of thought, and freedom of opportunity. Roosevelt declared: "Here they found life because here there was freedom to live."

The President then addressed the tens of thousands of immigrants who came in steerage. He paid tribute to the power of hope that had brought them to the New World; he honored their effort and devotion, which had made freedom safer, more far-reaching, and more capable of growth than ever. All were bound together more by hope for the future than by reverence for a common past. This heritage of hope helped forge a unity of purpose unmatched in the world.

★ FRANKLIN DELANO ROOSEVELT. Franklin Delano Roosevelt (1882–1945), the 32nd President of the United States, visited Liberty Island on October 28, 1936, to commemorate the fiftieth anniversary of the Statue of Liberty. Near the close of his first campaign for re-election, he urged his audience to rededicate themselves to the liberty and peace that the statue symbolized.

In 1937, the Army transferred its holdings on the island to the National Park Service. Two years later, a master plan was developed for the beautification of the island: All existing buildings, except Fort Wood, were to be demolished, removed, and, if necessary, replaced. World War II, however, caused these plans to be suspended; efforts to improve the island were not completed until the early 1950s, when the last prewar Army building was torn down.

The statue's lights were turned off throughout the war years as a precaution against possible enemy air or sea attack. There was, however, one notable exception: D-Day—June 6, 1944—the day that marked the Allied invasion of Europe. The following year victory in Europe restored the beacon of light to Liberty.

In 1952, the American Scenic and Historic Preservation Society, a private agency, suggested to the National Park Service the idea of constructing a museum of immigration within the very foundations of the statue. Pierre S. Du Pont III, spokesman for the project, stated that funds for the museum would be raised from the public, like the funds for the pedestal had been seventy years earlier. This museum would tell the story of how people—free, indentured, and slave—came to America from many nations since the early seventeenth century, and how they built this country from the Atlantic seacoast to the Pacific shores.

The Secretary of the Interior signed a cooperative agreement with the American Museum of Immigration, Inc. in 1955, one year after Ellis Island was officially closed as a gateway to America. The following year, fund-raising efforts for the museum were launched in earnest. During the next ten years, funds were collected for building the museum and materials were contributed to furnish it.

On May 11, 1965, President Lyndon Baines Johnson, pursuing a cause endorsed by assassinated President John F. Kennedy, visited Liberty Island. The purpose of the visit was to proclaim Ellis Island to be an integral part of the Statue of Liberty National Monument administered by the National Park Service. During the ceremony at the base of the statue, President Johnson called for passage of his proposed immigration bill, which would do away with the national origins quota scheme established by legislation in the 1920s. President Kennedy had long sought to reform discriminatory immigration laws and replace them with legislation "based on the skills of the applicants." Now President Johnson dramatically fulfilled Kennedy's wish. On October 3, 1965, Congress approved an immigration system that welcomed tens of thousands who would otherwise have been excluded.

★ LYNDON BAINES JOHNSON. Lyndon Baines Johnson (1908–73), the 36th President of the United States, also served as a member of the House of Representatives, as a member of the Senate, and as vice-president under President John F. Kennedy. Visiting Liberty Island on May 11, 1965, he signed into law legislation making Ellis Island part of the Statue of Liberty National Monument.

★ BICENTENNIAL OPERATION SAIL. During the festive celebrations of the nation's two hundredth anniversary in 1976, a flotilla of tall-masted sailing ships from around the world passed in review up the waters of New York harbor.

In 1972, the Museum of Immigration, headquartered in the pedestal of the Statue of Liberty, opened to the public. Soon after, the nation's Bicentennial celebrations focused renewed interest on America's rich and varied past. These years also evoked a dynamic commitment to preserve sites of historic significance throughout the land. The Statue of Liberty and Ellis Island were emotionally, as well as administratively, linked as important historic landmarks. Concerned people concurred that both sites needed repair and restoration.

A century after the American Committee and Joseph Pulitzer led the way to raise funds for the Liberty pedestal, a new and giant fund-raising effort was launched under the auspices of the Restore Ellis Island Committee and the Statue of Liberty/Ellis Island Centennial Commission. Their challenge is no less than to provide the financial and spiritual leadership in restoring these national treasures: Their mission is to preserve and protect these symbols of the American dream for generations to come, to kindle again in the hearts of all people the American promise to a world seeking hope and in search of liberty.

★ THE STATUE AT NIGHT: CONTEMPORARY SKYLINE. The Statue of Liberty is silhouetted at night against the towering skyline of lower Manhattan Island. The twin towers of the World Trade Center are directly behind the statue.

An Island of Hope

Within the shadow of the Statue of Liberty lies Ellis Island, immigration center for the Port of New York between 1892 and 1954. While Bartholdi's soaring statue was a world-renowned symbol of liberty and opportunity, the sight of Ellis Island and its low-lying buildings also stirred hope in the hearts and minds of the immigrant. At the same time, it aroused a variety of fears and uncertainties: fears about the outcome of the physical examination required of all new persons entering the country; fears over the questions that might be asked by the immigration officers; uncertainties about a new land, a new language, and new customs; uncertainties about finding a place to live or a job to sustain the immigrant and his family. Then there was also the inevitable and unspoken fear of possible rejection and deportation. Whatever prompted the American immigrants, they were brave, bold, and courageous men and women. They left familiar communities for a new land and a new people, in hopes of fulfilling their dreams. For some it was a dream of religious freedom; for others, a dream of political freedom. Many were driven by famine and economic hardship, and sought the opportunity to own their own house or some land or a farm.

★ IMMIGRANT GIRL. The warm, cheering, and confident features of an immigrant child suggest that she had no worries during the immigration process at Ellis Island. Between her thumb and forefinger, she holds her first American coin, a penny.

A Nation of Immigrants

The United States has always been a nation of immigrants. It was settled in its earliest days, the first decades of the seventeenth century, by English, Dutch, and French men and women. Other national groups soon arrived. In 1624 Walloons settled in New Amsterdam, while in the late 1630s Swedes established a community along the Delaware River. Near Philadelphia in 1682 a band of Welsh settled, followed a year or two later by Rhinelanders and Palatines who established Germantown. From Boston to New Rochelle, New York, and New York City, and southward to Charleston, South Carolina, French Huguenots settled, following the Edict of Nantes of October 18, 1685. Scots and Ulster-Scots began to enter the American colonies in 1689, although their main exodus from the old country lasted from 1714 to the outbreak of the Revolutionary War.

As early as 1710 German Palatines settled in the Hudson River Valley, later moving to the Schoharie Valley in Pennsylvania and then to the Mohawk River Valley in upper New York state. The heaviest period of German immigration to the American colonies occurred between 1727 and 1775, with major settlements at Savannah, Georgia (1735), Bethlehem, Pennsylvania (1744), and Winston-Salem, North Carolina (1753).

The period from 1827 to 1882 witnessed waves of Scandinavian, Irish, and German immigrants arriving in the young republic. During the 1840s and 1850s many Scandinavians settled in the Midwest, particularly Iowa, Illinois, Wisconsin, and Minnesota. Although

★ ELLIS ISLAND IN RELATION TO THE STATUE OF LIBERTY. Ellis Island stands in the very shadow of the Statue of Liberty. From nearly every vantage point in the harbor, as well as from Ellis Island, the immigrant could see Bartholdi's magnificent monument. The statue served as a symbol to the immigrant of new-found freedom, a sign that the years ahead in America would be ones of challenge and opportunity.

significant numbers of Irish began to immigrate to America in 1809, their flow was interrupted by the War of 1812. The mainstream of Irish immigration actually began in the 1820s, when the Irish represented 44 percent of the total number of immigrants and reached its peak after the great famine of 1846, when in 1851 some 221,253 Irish immigrants settled in America. German immigration was also substantial and rose during the 1830s to about 30 percent of total immigration. Poor farm conditions and the Revolution of 1848 prompted many Germans to leave their homeland and move into German colonies in New York, Baltimore, Cincinnati, St. Louis, and Milwaukee.

From 1830 through 1874 several states passed their own immigration laws, since the federal government did not regulate immigration in any way until 1875. An 1882 immigration statute limited immigration to the United States; it excluded the insane, convicts, and people who were thought likely to become indigents. Between 1880 and 1920 the people who composed the waves of immigration shifted significantly: in 1882, for example, 75 percent of the immigrants were from northern and western Europe, while by 1896 half were from southern and eastern Europe, and ten years later this proportion increased to 70 percent. However, immigration was eventually to be severely restricted by the quota laws of 1921 and 1924, and by the National Origins Act of 1929.

74 ★ CASTLE GARDEN, ABOUT 1850. Between 1855 and 1890, Castle Garden was a depot for immigration. It had been built (1807–11) as a fort, Fort Clinton. Ceded to New York City by the federal government in 1822, it was renamed and became a "resort" and concert hall. Its days as a concert hall were numbered as the city's immigration officials needed a waterfront location to serve as a port-of-entry. On August 1, 1855, Castle Garden processed its first immigrants. More than eight million immigrants passed through here during the next thirty-five years.

Gull Island

The native Americans named the small island in the harbor "Kilshk," or Gull Island, after its only and winged inhabitants. Gull Island was little more than a three-acre sand bank of mud and clay. After the Dutch established the colony of New Amsterdam, Gull Island's first European owner was the patroon, Mynher Michael Paauw, whose extensive landholdings stretched along the west bank of the Hudson River and included the present-day site of Hoboken. The island had earlier been purchased from the Indians by the governor of New Amsterdam on July 12, 1634, for "certain cargoes, or parcels of goods."

The island, which was used only for oyster fishing, changed hands many times during the colonial period. It was not until the Revolutionary War that the island was owned by one Samuel Ellis, whose name has since been linked to it. A merchant and farmer, Ellis passed the island on to his heirs at his death. It was from them that New York state purchased the island in 1808 and sold it in turn to the

federal government for the purpose of building a fort on it. New York harbor was being fortified by the federal government at that time, since the English were harassing American ships trading with West Indian ports.

Fortified just before the outbreak of the War of 1812, Ellis Island saw little action during the war. The Army and Navy seldom used the island. Occasionally the Army posted recruits there and in 1842 undertook to repair its installation, Fort Gibson. In 1835 the Navy opened a munitions depot on the island. By the late 1860s the Army had abandoned Fort Gibson, and the Navy expanded its powder magazine. The Navy continued to store munitions on the island until May 24, 1890, when it transferred its arsenal elsewhere. Shortly thereafter Ellis Island was transformed into an immigration center by the federal government, replacing the then-outworn facilities of Castle Garden located at the Battery on the southern tip of Manhattan Island.

Immigration Center

To transform Ellis Island into an immigration center took major construction: A channel had to be dredged to receive ferry boats; new docks and buildings had to be built. The main building, built of Georgia pine at a cost of $500,000, was opened on January 1, 1892. Two stories high, about 400 feet long and 150 feet wide (about the size of the grounds inside a football stadium), it looked on the outside like a Victorian seaside resort hotel. Baggage rooms filled the ground level. The great inspection hall was upstairs. Nearby on the grounds were hospital buildings, doctors' quarters, a bath house, laundry, kitchens, a dining hall, and a power plant. Some of Fort Gibson's old brick buildings had been converted for dormitory space, while the Navy's abandoned magazines housed records.

The immigrants faced new regulations. A comprehensive federal immigration law had been enacted by Congress in 1891. Now the federal government controlled and supervised all immigration procedures; the superintendent of the newly established Bureau of Immigration was charged with enforcing these stricter regulations.

Shortly after midnight on June 14, 1897, a fire broke out on the island. Soon the large wooden main building was engulfed in flames. By 1 o'clock the heavy slate roof collapsed; the building was in total ruins. Rescue boats rushed to the island, jamming the harbor. There were two hundred guards, doctors, and immigrants on the island at that time, and all were safely evacuated. Not one life was lost.

The Ellis Island depot was quickly rebuilt. The building that now arose from the timber ashes was fireproof: a brick exterior, concrete floors, iron railings, and metal appointments everywhere. The center served at once as hotel, hospital, prison, and transport station. The main building was 385 feet long and 165 feet wide, and contained

★ ORIGINAL ELLIS ISLAND CENTER. The first immigrant station built on Ellis Island was about 400 feet long and 150 feet wide. Officially opened on January 1, 1892, the two-story main building was built of Georgia pine at a cost of $500,000. On June 14, 1897, a disastrous fire totally destroyed the building.

★ NEW IMMIGRATION CENTER. A new depot at Ellis Island opened on December 17, 1900. Built—at a cost of $1,500,000—it was placed on the very same site as the earlier building.

enormous waiting rooms, offices, and examination rooms. Numerous smaller buildings nearby housed dormitories, hospital wards, a dining hall, the customs house, a telegraph station, docks, wharves, and residences for the staff.

On December 17, 1900, though still under construction, the center reopened. The first immigrants to be processed through the new depot were 654 Italian passengers who had crossed the Atlantic on the *Kaiser Wilhelm II*. Immediately after them came steerage passengers from the *Victoria*, the *Vincenzo Florio*, and the *Umbria*. On that first day, 2,251 immigrants passed through the portals of Ellis Island. For the next fifteen years—until the outbreak of World War I—men, women, and children of many ethnic and national backgrounds flooded the center, disembarking by the hundreds from nearly every ship that steamed from Europe through the Narrows of New York harbor.

EMIGRATION VESSEL.—BETWEEN DECKS.

★ CROWDED QUARTERS BELOW DECK. For more than two weeks, immigrants lived shoulder to shoulder in the steerage area below deck. Foul air, stale food, and filth surrounded them. Some passengers did not leave their bunks for days, unable to face the rolling motion of the ship or yet another meal of lukewarm soup, boiled potatoes, and stringy beef.

★ IMMIGRANTS PACKED ABOARD SHIPS. Packed in steerage aboard passenger ships, immigrants had little room. This crowded deck illustrates the conditions they endured crossing the Atlantic to America. Nearly all privacy and most dignity were lost within the confines of a rolling ship on a churning sea.

Passing Through the Portal

Crossing the North Atlantic was seldom smooth. Wind, rain, and high seas gave a rolling, pitching motion to the steamships of the day. The poorer immigrants were usually packed into the bow or steerage sections of the ship. They spent much of the voyage lying cramped in narrow bunks, surrounded by the stench of unwashed bodies, the odors of seasickness, and the smells of old food. Separated from family and friends as well as the familiar sights of a well-known city, town, or farm, they must have brooded on the uncertainty of their future during those next few days and weeks aboard ship.

Entering the Narrows has always been a spectacular sight, whether for Giovanni De Verrazano or Henry Hudson or Auguste Bartholdi. It was no less so for the millions of immigrants who entered during those decades. Surrounded by scores of steamships at anchor and flying the flags of many nations, the immigrants could spot the church spires and the commercial and residential buildings of lower Manhattan and Brooklyn. On their left as they rounded the Battery stood Bartholdi's sacred lady of the harbor, her torch uplifted, touching the heavens. Beyond the statue and in her shadow stood the red-brick buildings of Ellis Island. The immigrants' ship usually docked at one of the Hudson River piers that lined lower Manhattan. First-class and cabin-class passengers disembarked first, passing through customs and immigration with little delay. The well-to-do immigrants who could afford cabin-class passage merely walked down the ship's gangplank and into their newly adopted homeland. Next, it was the poorer immigrants, turn to leave the ship and wait on the dock for the ferry to carry them back down river to Ellis Island.

★ STATUE OF LIBERTY IN SIGHT. As the steamships entered New York harbor, immigrants strained to catch their first sight of the lady with the torch. "This is America!" The long journey was over; Liberty welcomed her new children home.

★ FERRY BOAT WITH IMMIGRANTS; IMMIGRANTS ON FERRY. Immigrants crowded the decks
and railings of the ferry boats as they traveled from arrival piers to Ellis Island.
The passengers traveled on the upper deck, while their baggage was loaded
onto the lower deck. Here we also see an Italian immigrant family being
transported from the Hudson River docks to Ellis Island.

★ CLIMBING THE STAIRCASE TO THE GREAT HALL. With luggage and baskets in hand, a group of Slavic immigrants climb the staircase to the Great Hall in the Main Building at Ellis Island. Medical inspectors waited at the top of the stairs and quickly checked to see if an immigrant had heart or respiratory difficulties or was otherwise obviously handicapped.

★ ARRIVAL ON ELLIS ISLAND DOCKS. Laden with suitcases, backpacks, and bundles, the immigrants disembarked at Ellis Island from their brief, fifteen-minute ferry boat trip. They then walked to the red-brick Main Building to begin the process of inspection.

On the island, the immigrants—laden with bundles, baggage, and children in their hands—were greeted by strange shouts, commands, and shoves by guards. Standing together, numbered tags pinned to their chests, the immigrants awaited their tests by examining doctors of the United States Public Health Service. Searching for breathing problems or physical disabilities, the physicians looked at each immigrant's face, hair, neck, and hands and through an interpreter asked questions about the immigrant's age or work to test alertness. Everybody—men, women, and children—were asked their names to determine whether or not they were deaf or dumb. Suspected heart trouble, mental illness, skin infection, tuberculosis, physical disabilities, or trachoma would cause the immigrant to be rejected, detained on the island, and deported. Family members could be separated—some accepted, some rejected—and painful decisions about staying or returning with the rejected loved one had to be made on the spot.

Each immigrant was asked a list of twenty-nine questions. "Who paid for your ship's fare?" "Do you have a job waiting for you?" "What kind of work do you do?" "Is anyone meeting you?" "Where are you going?" "Can you read and write?" "Have you ever been in prison?" "How much money do you have?" "Show it to me." "Where did you get it?" After satisfactorily completing the questioning, a landing card was issued and the immigrant was officially admitted into the United States.

★ IMMIGRANTS IN PENS; WAITING. At the top of the staircase was the Great Hall or Registry Hall, over 200 feet long, 100 feet wide, and with a 56-foot vaulted ceiling. Immigrants passed through a maze of passageways with iron-pipe railings, called "the pens." In 1911, the iron railings were removed and replaced by wooden benches.

The atmosphere at Ellis Island was all too often marked by unfairness, rudeness, and dishonesty. In the restaurant, operated by concession, the tableware and bowls were seldom washed; restaurant employees frequently robbed immigrants and then forced them to work in the kitchen. At the money exchange, it was not uncommon for the clerk to cheat an immigrant in the transaction; while in the Registry Hall, inspectors were known to suggest that clearance would be quicker if their palms were crossed with money. Immigrants who carried large amounts of cash were sometimes detained without cause until they "saw reason." Pretty girls who would agree to a rendezvous later at a Manhattan hotel were speedily admitted. Once the immigrant had the prized landing card in hand, they remained prey for the restaurant operator who sold expensive box lunches and the railroad agents who overcharged for tickets. Not until Theodore Roosevelt became President in 1901 were the rampant abuses at Ellis Island attacked and reforms in conditions and procedures instituted. Under Roosevelt, the goal was to run Ellis Island as a hospitable service center for the new American, not as a pool for thievery by concessionaires and their staffs.

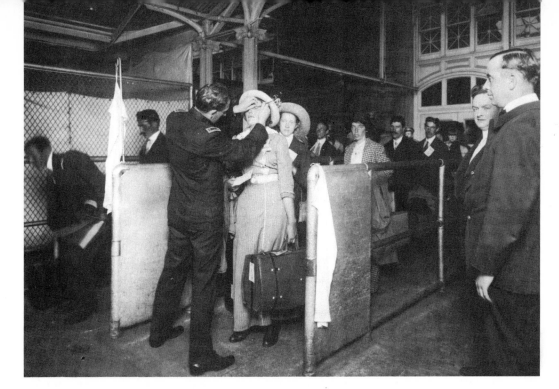

★ EYE EXAMINATION; IMMIGRANT CHILDREN. Everyone passing through Ellis Island underwent an eye examination. The inspectors searched for any eye infections, especially trachoma, which was the cause of more than half the medical detentions. The variety of dress reminds us of the many lands from which the children came.

★ MONEY EXCHANGE. The signs above the cage read *Cambia Valuta, Lamiana Pienendzy, Wechselgeschäft, Money Exchange*. The first stop after passing through the immigration station was to this booth to exchange gold, silver, and European currencies for American dollars. The official rates of exchange were posted each day on a blackboard by the cashiers.

★ RAILROAD TICKETS. Railroad tickets to cities and towns across the country were sold by agents. With tickets in their hands, the immigrants heading elsewhere than to New York City sat in the large Waiting Room in areas marked for each railroad line. They were then ferried to the terminal stations in Jersey City or Hoboken.

★ ARMENIAN JEW. The haunting features of this unknown, unnamed, travel-weary Armenian Jew mirrors the imageless millions of men and women who passed through the gateway of Ellis Island. He had traveled from a distant, turbulent section of the Middle East in his search for liberty.

Only a very small number of persons who walked up the grand stairway to the examination hall were detained and deported. By law anybody who was a known criminal, a prostitute, mentally ill, or suffering from a contagious disease could be denied admission to the United States. A Board of Special Inquiry heard each detainee's appeal, as well as the testimony of relatives and lawyers. If ordered by the Board to leave, the detainee could appeal to the Secretary of Commerce and Labor in Washington, who often sustained the detainee's appeal or ordered a new hearing on the matter. Those who were to be deported were usually detained on Ellis Island for only two or three weeks until a ship of the line that brought them to America arrived in port and could return them to the port from which they came.

It is estimated that between 12 and 16 million people climbed the grand stairway and passed through the corridors and inspection halls of Ellis Island. The exact number is uncertain, since the records of immigrant arrivals are incomplete. We do know, however, that nearly all immigrants successfully assimilated themselves into the communities in which they settled: the tenements of the lower east side of New York City or similar neighborhoods in other large cities throughout the United States; or in the small towns of Illinois, Iowa, and Kansas; or on the farms of Minnesota, North Dakota, and Nebraska.

88

★ ON THE WAY BACK TO THE DOCKS. The immigration procedures completed— the eye and physical examinations, the twenty-nine rapid-fire questions answered, money exchanged and, if necessary, railroad tickets purchased— the immigrants were now at dockside again for the short, final journey to New York City or New Jersey.

★ BLACK WOMEN. A small but significant stream of black immigrants entered the United States, particularly from various Caribbean islands, before World War I. They came to America's shores to escape colonial exploitation.

★ ALMOST THERE. From the docks of Ellis Island, New York City's skyline looms large. The ferry boat carried the immigrants to the piers of Manhattan as quickly as possible. The passage from the Old World was finished; the New World journey had only begun.

A Procession of Heroes

Many immigrants who passed through the Ellis Island gateway have notably enriched the social, cultural, and economic fabric of America. Irving Berlin (1888–   ), songwriter extraordinaire, was born in Temun, Siberia, and came to the United States in 1893. Without benefit of formal music training, he composed such popular classics as "Alexander's Ragtime Band" and "Easter Parade." The great Notre Dame football coach, Knute Rockne, arrived in 1893 from Norway. A year later the Vienna-born Felix Frankfurter arrived, destined to make his mark as a distinguished professor at the Harvard Law School and as a justice of the United States Supreme Court. Samuel Goldwyn and Spyros Skouras, two giants of the Hollywood movie industry, reached Ellis Island in 1896 and 1910 respectively; while the film and play director, Elia Kazan, arrived in 1913. Future labor and industrial leaders also entered America through this portal: from Scotland in 1902, Philip Murray, second president of the C.I.O.; and from Poland via Siberia in 1911, David Dubinsky, founder of the International Ladies Garment Workers Union. William S. Knudsen, who was to head General Motors, reached Ellis Island in 1900 from Denmark. And Father Edward Flanagan, the architect and spiritual head of Boys Town in Nebraska, arrived from Ireland some four years later.

World War I put an end to the flood of men, women, and children who entered the United States through Ellis Island. In 1914, 878,052 persons passed through the immigration center, while during the following year—the first full year of fighting in Europe—only 178,416 arrived; by 1919 the number had declined to a mere 26,731, or the equivalent of four- to five-days' arrivals during the prewar period. By now there was no need for an army of employees at Ellis Island. Some were transferred to other federal posts, while some were given long leaves of absence. The enormous Registry Hall was deserted, the docks were quiet, and the baggage room was empty.

During World War I, Ellis Island doubled as an internment camp for German merchant crewmen who had been arrested in the harbors of New York City and London. Nearly 1,150 of these officers and men were quartered in the baggage and dormitory buildings at any one time. During the course of the war, about 2,200 Germans were imprisoned on the island.

★ KNUTE KENNETH ROCKNE. Knute Kenneth Rockne (1888–1931) migrated from Norway in 1893 and settled in Chicago. At the University of Notre Dame, he excelled in football, and later (1918–31) served as its legendary coach.

★ FATHER EDWARD J. FLANAGAN. Father Edward J. Flanagan (1886–1948) emigrated from Ireland in 1904. A Roman Catholic priest and founder of Boys Town, Nebraska, he rehabilitated the lives of hundreds of abandoned and neglected boys.

★ IRVING BERLIN. Born in Temun, Russia (1888–   ), Irving Berlin is one of the most distinguished of America's songwriters and composers. He became a U.S. citizen and served in the Army during World War I.

Closing the Door

At the close of World War I, many Americans were eager to see the flow of immigrants severely restricted. It was an era that favored prohibition of immigration as well as of liquor. The war had rekindled a long-standing fear, even hatred, of foreigners. As early as 1849 in New York City, a secret oath-bound society, calling itself the Order of the Star-Spangled Banner, protested the rise of Irish Catholic and German immigration. The same nativist sentiments gave rise to the Know Nothing political party in the 1850s and revived again in the 1880s. The Chinese Exclusion Act of 1882 prohibited Chinese laborers from entering the United States for ten years. The American Protective Association was founded in 1887 in Clinton, Louisiana, as an anti-Catholic, anti-immigrant organization, and reached its maximum influence by 1896.

Still another nativist secret society was organized in Georgia in 1915, adopting the ominous name of a post-Civil War, anti-Reconstruction terrorist society—the Ku Klux Klan. This group directed its hatred against American-born Negroes, as well as against immigrant Jews and Catholics. Organizations such as the Immigration Restriction League based in New England began to broadcast by printed word as well as by mouth that mass immigration should stop. In their opinion, the United States could not absorb one more "new"

★ LOOKING BACKWARD: NATIVISM. Nativism has erupted from time to time throughout the American experience; it seems to come in cycles and is often marked by hysteria and irrationality. Its generally stated political purpose is to safeguard "pure" American nationality from the threat of foreign influences and "contamination." At various times, antagonisms were directed against Catholics, Jews, and other ethnic groups; also against the poor and unskilled workers who competed for certain jobs. All social, political, and economic evils were piled upon the shoulders of the immigrants or their fathers. The nativist solution was at all times simply to close the door of further immigration.

immigrant from eastern and southern European. The efforts of such nativist groups, coupled with those of organized labor, who wanted to terminate new competition for factory jobs—in a time when America faced high unemployment, collapsing farm prices, and high inflation— led to a drastic revision of the immigration laws. Ironically, the nativists were descendants of earlier immigrants; and the labor leaders may have been immigrants themselves, and they certainly represented the immigrant constituency that made up the majority of America's labor force.

In 1917 President Woodrow Wilson vetoed a law passed by Congress that would significantly reduce the number of immigrants. Wilson declared that the proposed legislation, which included a literacy test, would destroy the image of the United States as a land of the free. Furthermore, he avowed it was unfair that those who came seeking opportunity were now not to be admitted unless they already had one of the chief opportunities which they were seeking in the first place, the opportunity of education. He attacked the proposed literacy test as restrictive not selective, since it excluded "those to whom the opportunities of elementary education had been denied, without regard to their character, their purposes, or their natural capacity." This former university president saw his veto overruled by an opposition Congress. The new Immigration Act become law on February 5, 1917, remaining in force until 1952.

94

★ WOODROW WILSON. Woodrow Wilson (1856–1924), 28th President of the United States (1913–19), previously served as president of Princeton University and governor of New Jersey. Wilson was awarded the Nobel Peace Prize in 1919 for his work at the Versailles Peace Conference.

Although there were new restrictions on immigration and the literacy test had to be passed for admission to the United States, the number of arrivals in New York began to climb again. In 1920 over 200,000 immigrants entered the United States, over 500,000 in 1921. Entrance examinations were now so detailed that the process took much longer than before. The staff at Ellis Island was overworked, the facilities crammed. Since the literacy test had failed to reduce the flow of immigration, particularly from the war-ravaged countries of Europe, a new, more powerful method of exclusion was enacted in 1921, the Quota System. This new immigration law limited the number of immigrants from any country in any one year to three percent of the number of its natives residing in the United States in 1910, with a minimum quota of 100. An annual ceiling of 358,000 immigrants was also set. This plan meant that the largest quotas were assigned to the oldest immigrant groups—those from northern Europe—whereas the number of people allowed from the newer groups—those from eastern and southern Europe—were reduced to a mere fraction of their pre-World War I arrivals.

Three years later an even more restrictive law based on the same quota principle superseded the harsh 1921 Immigration Act. The Johnson-Reed Act of 1924 limited the entire number of European immigrants to 150,000 and fixed quotas for individual countries at one-sixth of one percent of people of those origins living in the United

States in 1920. Italy's quota was thereby decreased, for example, from 42,057 (1921 Act) to 3,845 (1924 Act) people a year. The total number of immigrants allowed under the 1924 law was reduced from 350,000 to 164,000 per year; and the Act of 1924 essentially excluded all Asians, a fact bitterly resented by the Japanese, among others.

The 1924 Johnson-Reed Act also included another provision that proved to have a far-reaching effect on Ellis Island. The law required all potential immigrants to be examined at U.S. Consular Offices throughout Europe before embarking to go to America. At these centers, consular officers were empowered to issue visas to men, women, and children who were found to be acceptable. It was the task of consular officers to fill the various national quotas, issuing no more than ten percent of the available visas in any one month. The purpose of this new screening system was to end the first-come, first-served basis of processing immigrants used earlier by the steamship companies, a procedure that inevitably led to many tearful disappointments in American ports of entry.

Soon after the 1924 Immigration Act was adopted, traffic through Ellis Island subsided to a trickle. Although it remained the chief immigration center in the United States proper, the island's role was irreversibly changing. Immigration inspectors and public health doctors, now stationed at U.S. consulates overseas, undertook the initial examinations of immigrants before they sailed for New York: The flow of traffic was steady month after month. The staff at Ellis Island made a final perfunctory check of all passengers as each ship entered New York harbor, but possession of a United States visa virtually guaranteed admission. Few were now turned away at this final gateway to America.

The decreasing traffic flowing through Ellis Island allowed time for long-deferred repairs to be made at the immigration center. Modern plumbing was installed, and new beds and mattresses were placed in the dormitories. Yet as dust began to settle in the now deserted rooms of the Ellis Island depot, Washington officials were already beginning to refer to the immigration center as an economic problem.

A final revision of the "national origins" quota system went into effect on July 1, 1929. The maximum number of *all* admissions to the United States was now reduced to only 150,000 people annually. This, combined with the new, more restrictive quota rules, was a deliberate attempt to permanently set the ethnic and racial mix of the American nation. New quotas were calculated on an analysis of the national origins of the population, native and foreign-born, as noted in the 1920 federal census. Determining the number of persons to be admitted each year was a complex process. The number of each nationality to be admitted in any one year was to be in the same proportion to 150,000 as the number of that national origin in the United States in 1920 was to the total population. Accordingly, after July 1, 1929, only 6,524 Polish and 2,712 Russian immigrants could enter each year, as contrasted with 65,721 from Great Britain. The outcome was obvious: Immigrants from eastern and southern European nations had to wait for years to receive a visa, while the British never once filled their quota.

In October 1929, Wall Street collapsed and the Great Depression began. Factories and stores closed; millions of workers lost their jobs. In foreign cities and towns, would-be immigrants grasped that American streets were not paved with gold. There was no need to struggle to seek entry to a country where a man or woman was neither welcomed nor wanted and where work could no longer be found.

During the 1930s the chief role of Ellis Island was to serve as the country's center for deporting unwanted persons. The number of arrested immigrants expelled through the island far outnumbered the immigrants arriving in New York: For example, in 1932 nearly twenty thousand persons were deported, compared with three thousand who passed through Ellis Island en route to a new life in the United States. Besides the deportees, there were many more thousands of men and women who of their own free will chose to leave the United States to return to the countries of their birth. During the depth of the Depression in 1933, 127,660 people left the United States, while only 23,068 new immigrants arrived. The era of the great migration from Europe to America was over. The door to America was virtually shut.

A Final Flurry

Economic stagnation in the United States of the 1930s was matched by economic troubles in Europe and elsewhere around the world. Yet the rise of Adolph Hitler and the resulting political turmoil in Europe reversed the declining trend of immigration. From 1933 through the war years of World War II, some 250,000 refugees entered the United States. Many were Jewish or were political opponents of fascism. Each had to produce guarantees that he or she would not fall on the public welfare rolls. Their numbers included the physicists Albert Einstein and Enrico Fermi, the scientists Leo Szilard, Edward Teller, George Gamow and Theodore Van Karman, the writer Thomas Mann, and the Protestant theologian Paul Tillich. Not since the turbulence of the 1848 revolution in Germany had so many intellectuals sought refuge in the United States.

★ ALBERT EINSTEIN. Albert Einstein (1879–1955) emigrated from Nazi Germany to the United States in 1932. A physicist of gigantic intellect, he was awarded the Nobel Prize in physics in 1921.

★ ENRICO FERMI. Enrico Fermi (1901–54) came to the United States in 1939 from his native Rome. Another scientific genius, he received a Nobel Prize in physics in 1938.

★ SPYROS P. SKOURAS. A pioneer of the motion picture industry, Spyros P. Skouras (1893–1971) emigrated from Greece to the United States in 1910. He rose from a job as a busboy in St. Louis to the presidency of Twentieth Century-Fox Film Corporation.

98

★ ELLIS ISLAND. Ellis Island was at its peak of activity during the years between 1900 and 1914. Immigrants fleeing Czarist Russia, Italy, Austria-Hungary, Germany, Ireland, and Poland passed in their millions through this portal to America. In 1907 alone, 1,004,756 newcomers arrived at Ellis Island. An average of five thousand immigrants a day were processed, seven days a week. On April 17, 1907—the most active day of all—11,745 immigrants were admitted.

At the end of World War II and under the leadership of President Harry S Truman, the United States Congress was asked to facilitate the entrance of displaced persons from war-ravaged Europe. By an act of Congress on June 25, 1948, visas were authorized for the admission of 205,000 European displaced persons, including 3,000 nonquota orphans. The number was later increased to 341,000 visas. Certain discriminatory provisions were eliminated from the immigration law and new categories of expellees and war orphans added to the rolls.

However, the McCarran-Walter Act of 1952, which was passed over the veto of President Truman, codified U.S. immigration laws and generally retained the provisions of the 1924 legislation regarding maximum immigration, as well as the quota system. This Act did remove the ban on immigration of Asian and Pacific peoples, while also providing screening measures to keep out subversives. Revision of this Act is under consideration.

In November 1954, Ellis Island bid a final farewell to its last immigrant and its last detainee. The Immigration Service offices were closed and moved to lower Manhattan. The following March the

immigration center was declared "surplus property" by the federal
government, and in 1955 the General Services Administration
advertised the island for sale to a commercial buyer at a value of
$6,500,000. Thirty-five buildings occupied the island, including:
fourteen office buildings, eleven storage facilities, dormitories, cafeteria,
dining room, laundry, power house, and post office. No sale took place.
Ten years later, after its buildings had been much ravaged by neglect
and vandals, President Lyndon B. Johnson on May 11, 1965, declared
Ellis Island and the Statue of Liberty a national park.

An era was over. A once wide-open door had been closed. Once-
bustling docks were now still. Ellis Island had borne the footprints,
witnessed the tears, and heard the laughter of millions since its
opening on January 1, 1892. Ever in the reflected light of her majestic
neighbor, Ellis Island had served as a final checkpoint, a final hurdle
on the way to America. She had more importantly served as the
gateway into a life of hope. Her guests had passed through by the
millions in their search of liberty and in their quest of the American
dream.

★ ELLIS ISLAND IN DECAY: REGISTRY HALL. Deserted since 1954, the Registry Hall is today in decay and disrepair: no shouts heard, no commands given, no questions asked by impersonal immigration inspectors. The cacophony of immigrant voices, dazzled and bewildered by unfamiliar surroundings and proceedings, is now stilled.

★ ELLIS ISLAND IN DECAY: FERRY BOAT. Tied to its moorings at the slip on Ellis Island when the immigration depot was closed in 1954, the ferry boat *Ellis Island* has not been kindly treated by time. Three decades of decay, ice, and tides have scuttled the old vessel. During more than fifty years, she had logged over 1,000,000 nautical miles shuttling passengers back and forth across the harbor.

A Search for Liberty

Liberty is at once the strongest of human dreams and, yet, the most fragile of human experiences. In their search for liberty, men and women will foment revolutions and cross vast oceans and trackless continents. Yet once achieved, even in part, liberty can soon be lost to the bondage of petty rules and bureaucratic indifference. To gain liberty one must risk all; to retain liberty requires unceasing vigilance.

In the never-ending search for liberty, monumental battles have been won or lost throughout the history of mankind. There are memorials—such as our beloved Statue of Liberty—that remind us at what cost these fragile liberties were won. And there are everyday skirmishes to preserve and enhance those liberties. The enemy we face is not so much the evil person, as it is the good person who has become bored with liberty and does little in its defense. Liberty dies silently and surely when free people no longer care.

Each generation marks its own battlefield upon which it must perform its acts of valor in defense of liberty. What one generation wins at great personal price can be lost by the next generation for a mere pittance. *In Search of Liberty* is not only a celebration of liberty—and America's national symbols of this great spiritual and social treasure—but it is a call to daily rededication to hold these liberties fast and to extend them across the range of human experience.

★ To gain liberty one must risk all; to retain liberty requires unceasing vigilance.

A Gift from the Old World

The Statue of Liberty embodies the yearning for freedom and opportunity that the very name "America" has come to mean to millions the world over. The dreams of these millions of ordinary people who find the doors to freedom and opportunity locked shut against them in their own native lands can be best summed up in the phrase "if only I or my children could get to America!" Our grand Lady of the Harbor evokes their hopes and dreams beyond measure. Indeed, this vision of Liberty personified reverberates more forcefully within our hearts and minds than ten thousand speeches in praise of freedom.

First and foremost, the Statue was intended to commemorate two of history's great milestones in the ceaseless search for liberty—the Declaration of Independence and the successful conclusion of the American War of Independence. The statue was a gift *from* the people of one nation—France—whose diplomatic and military partnership in the War of Independence helped achieve the final success at Yorktown. The Statue was also a gift *to* the people of another nation—the United States of America—whose striving for liberty and social justice inspired the French in their own search for "liberté, egalité et fraternité."

Thomas Jefferson, chief author of the Declaration of Independence, crystalized mankind's universal yearning for liberty when he spoke of those self-evident truths that the laws and government of a new American nation would attempt to nurture in its political life: the equality of all people; their inalienable rights to life, liberty and the pursuit of happiness; the belief that governments exist to secure these rights for all citizens; and that governments derive their just powers from the consent of the people they govern. Such a view of liberty and government was novel and revolutionary in an age when mankind had known only monarchs and marquises, kings and despots, tsars and tyrants.

During the first hundred years of the American experience, these liberties were secured and enlarged for more people and for a longer period of time than ever before in history. Notwithstanding America's own dark side of slavery, of uprooting and pillaging of her native Americans, of economic exploitation and opportunism, this nation was still the haven to which Europe's oppressed and needy fled in great human waves.

★ *Not like the brazen giant of Greek fame,*
  With conquering limbs astride from land to land;
  Here at our sea-washed, sunset gates shall stand
  A mighty woman with a torch, whose flame
  Is the imprisoned lightning, and her name
  Mother of Exiles. . . .

Led by Professor Édouard René Lefebvre de Laboulaye, a small band of Frenchmen enlisted the enthusiastic commitment of Frédéric Auguste Bartholdi to bring the vision of a statue commemorating Liberty into a reality. The initial name given to the statue was *Liberty Enlightening the World.* The statue was not merely to serve as a monumental work honoring a century-old conflict, but also to embody the heady spirit of Liberty as it evolved in both the French and American arenas, serving as an inspiration for all nations, for all peoples, for all times.

Bartholdi explored a variety of visual symbols for his heroic work. Among them was Columbia, a feminine personification of America. Named after Christopher Columbus, Columbia was given the quiet dignity of a seated classical goddess. She had appeared on American coins and official seals, but she seemed too sedate for Bartholdi. Conversely, Delacroix's passionate painting of *Liberty Leading the People* shows Liberty in the form of a vigorous woman, rifle in one hand and Tricolor in the other, leading the people forward against the barricade. Her clothes are half-torn away, her face suffused with light, and the people follow in adoration and abandon, for her cause is theirs. Although this concept of Liberty became in time a widely used symbol for the French nation and people, Bartholdi wanted his statue to convey less passion. In successive models, he evolved the statue in her final form: a serene but forceful woman in classical garb, with an upheld torch of freedom, a diadem of light, with chains of bondage broken, and a sacred tablet inscribed with the date of the Declaration of Independence.

We have had a century to take this Lady of Light into our very hearts and make her an integral part of our own national spirit and consciousness. That we have done so speaks eloquently of the insight and integrity of Bartholdi's vision.

★ *JUDGE'S* SALUTE TO BARTHOLDI. The illustrated weekly, *Judge,* saluted the work of the Monument Committee, which was responsible for the raising of the Statue of Liberty. The members of the committee are shown: back row from left to right, Richard M. Hunt, Frederick A. Potts, Joseph Pulitzer, Frédéric Auguste Bartholdi, Richard Butler, Parke Godwin, V. Mumford Moore, and Henry F. Spalding; front row left to right, Levi P. Morton, Joseph W. Drexel, William M. Evarts, and Maj. Gen. Charles P. Stone.

★ LA LIBERTÉ GUIDANT LE PEUPLE. Bartholdi's use of a traditional heroic woman as symbolic of the spirit of Liberty was in contrast to the classic work, *La Liberté Guidant Le Peuple*, painted in 1830 by his fellow Frenchman, Delacroix. Carrying the Tricolor and a flintlock, Delacroix's woman climbs over the corpses that have fallen in the struggle for freedom. She is not the distant Greek or Roman goddess, but a woman of the people in the midst of armed revolt.

★ BARTHOLDI'S MODELS. As Bartholdi's conception of the Statue of Liberty evolved, he fashioned a number of models, including the two shown here that were made in 1875.

A National Symbol

People came to America seeking some kind of liberty that circumstances in the Old World denied them. It may have been the liberty to worship according to the dictates of conscience. Or it may have been the liberty of opportunity, whether you were a younger son of a prosperous family whose opportunity was blocked by older brothers who had inherited the family possessions, or whether you were a penniless son of an eastern European serf with little promise in life but hunger and poverty. Or it may have been the liberty of political freedom, whether you came from a country in which the state supported pogroms or from one in which you faced denial of your civil rights merely because you owed a small debt. Or it may have been the liberty of adequate food, whether the potatoes failed and your family starved or your country was overrun by war and the economy collapsed. Or it may have been even the liberty to dream dreams and try to bring them into reality.

The Statue of Liberty has come to symbolize all these quests. Although immigration from the Old World started in the late 1500s, over half of the population of the United States today is directly related to immigrants who passed by the Statue of Liberty and through Ellis Island during the six decades from 1892 to 1954. These immigrants could see the statue as they underwent their processing at Ellis Island: She embodied their quest for liberty, and the drama of that moment has become a part of the spiritual heritage of each immigrant family.

Every summer New York harbor is crowded with pilgrims who come from all over the United States to pay homage to their family's passage to America. The story of over one hundred million Americans literally cannot be told apart from the story of the Statue of Liberty and Ellis Island.

★ ELLIS ISLAND AND THE NEW YORK SKYLINE. Ellis Island is inseparably linked with the Statue of Liberty as symbolic companions in the search for liberty. Over one hundred million Americans today are descended from the twelve million immigrants who sailed past the statue and passed through Ellis Island.

The Quest for Religious Freedom

Many immigrants came to America in search of the freedom to worship as they wished. In some countries the state had formally adopted a particular religion, and those who held to other practices and beliefs were often physically and economically persecuted and abused. More often civil rights were withheld from them. Frequently disruptive and criminal elements in these countries could persecute the dissenters without state interference and often with state sanction.

Early in the American experience, colonists seeking religious liberty came from England, whose rulers preferred having these dissidents in the far-off New World than in nearby Bristol or Bedford. Puritans and Separatists came to Massachusetts and settled throughout New England. Presbyterians occupied the Middle Atlantic region. The Society of Friends established Pennsylvania, and many of its members lived in New Jersey. Huguenots fled the bloody massacres

in France for New York City and Charlestown, South Carolina. Small German pietist groups left a Germany that persecuted them for a refuge in a Pennsylvania that offered them tolerance and opportunity: the Mennonites and Amish to Lancaster, the Moravian Brethren to Bethlehem and Nazareth, and the Schwenckfelders to Montgomery County. Fleeing wars in Germany that had strong religious overtones were Lutherans, Reformed, and some Roman Catholics. Maryland was established as a colony that provided a haven for Roman Catholics during a period of great conflict between Anglicans and Roman Catholics in England. It was only after the American Revolution—and the overthrow of British rule—that Roman Catholics could worship publicly throughout the new nation.

The Constitution of the United States was adopted by the 13 original states only on the proviso that the first ten amendments would be concurrently adopted. Although the Constitution does not speak of religion—except to insist that "no religious test shall be required as a qualification to any office or public trust under the United States"—the very first amendment guarantees full religious liberty: "Congress shall make no law respecting an establishment of religion, or prohibiting the free exercise thereof . . ." Nothing is more profoundly American than this bedrock Constitutional guarantee of the rights of the individual to personal faith and practice and this affirmation that this nation is unalterably committed to religious pluralism.

In the two centuries since America officially separated the state from religion, waves of immigrants seeking religious liberty continued to arrive. Sephardic Jews settled in cities along the Eastern Seaboard. Ashkenazic Jews came in great waves from eastern Europe in the late nineteenth century. Tens of thousands of Jews came from Germany to escape anti-Semitic laws in the 1860s to 1880s, to be followed in the 1930s by thousands seeking refuge from Hitler's oppression. Hundreds of thousands of Jews from the rural areas and cities located between the Baltic and the Black Sea—from Russia, the Austro-Hungarian Empire, Romania, and Poland—came to the United States to escape tsarist pogroms, poverty, and intensified persecution to find religious freedom in the United States.

Whenever groups of people came, for whatever reason, they brought with them their religious beliefs, practices and institutions. The American Roman Catholic Church is a wondrous amalgam of Irish, Italian, French, Hispanic, Portuguese, Polish, German, and scores of other national Catholic histories, traditions, ecclesiastics,

★ IMMIGRANTS RECEIVING BIBLES. Representatives of the New York Bible Society distributed copies of the Bible and religious information to immigrants as they departed from Ellis Island.

languages, orders, and concerns mixed together in one multilithic body. The Greeks brought their national Orthodox Church, as did the Romanians and the Russians. The Swedes brought their national Lutheran Church, as did the Germans and the Norwegians. There are even two Dutch Reformed bodies: one springing from the original Dutch settlement of colonial times, and the second entering with the Dutch immigrants of the mid-1800s with their own re-Reformed Church. Immigrants from Asia have introduced Buddhism, Taoism, and Hinduism; and Islam has come from North Africa, the Middle East, and central Asia.

The Quest for Political Freedom

Deciding to cast off the yoke of British rule was relatively easy for American patriots; but actually casting off the yoke itself was far more difficult, involving seven long years of war and sacrifice. Yet securing the freedoms fought for in the form and practice of a just government was the most difficult task of all. Many a revolution has been won, but the cause for which it was fought lost in its aftermath.

America was blessed by the caliber and talents of those Founding Fathers who met together in Philadelphia in 1787 to give birth to a new nation and a new form of government. These Founding Fathers were not without experience or wisdom. Each had been active

★ *"... Give me your tired, your poor,*
Your huddled masses yearning to breathe free,
The wretched refuse of your teeming shore,
Send these, the homeless, tempest-tost to me.
I lift my lamp beside the golden door!"

in colonial affairs before the Revolution, and each was trusted by his state for his judgment and good sense. They had seen the new nation begin to founder under the Articles of Confederation, and they wanted to strengthen a national government without endangering local government and individual rights. The Constitution they created during those hot summer months was ratified by the states and has stood the test of two centuries. The United States of America is in fact the oldest democratic republic in the world, and has preserved intact those liberties for which the War of Independence was fought.

The Founding Fathers had a fundamental distrust of governmental power in any form. They were well-versed in political history and philosophy. They had felt the abuse of power by their English rulers; they had seen political power corrupt good men when one person or one group was allowed too much power. So in Philadelphia that summer nearly two hundred years ago, they devised a system of government that separated and divided power: executive from judicial from legislative, local from national, large state from small state. Every exercise of power by one branch or division of government could be held in check by the power granted to another branch or division. No person could become so powerful as to have his way without check; and no majority could exercise so much power as to oppress any minority ... the blatant exception to this principle was formally corrected by the Emancipation Proclamation, which outlawed slavery some eighty years later.

Civil liberty has grown steadily for our citizens under this Constitution. The only general constraint in the exercise of liberty is the constraint against abusing the freedom of others in the exercise of one's own freedom. American civil liberties are safeguarded for all generations:

> We, the People of the United States, in Order to form a more perfect Union, establish Justice, insure domestic Tranquility, provide for the common defense, promote the general Welfare, and *secure the Blessings of Liberty to ourselves and our Posterity*, do ordain and establish this Constitution for the United States of America.

Preamble to the Constitution

What are some of these civil liberties? A review of some of the provisions of the Constitution suggest the extent to which our Founding Fathers bequeathed to us an inheritance of political freedom.

* Even the President of the United States can be impeached if he abuses his powers (I,3).

* No member of Congress shall have any executive position in government, thus avoiding a possible conflict of interest (I,6).

* No one can be held in custody indefinitely without cause (I,9).

* No one can be imprisoned for doing something that was legal at the time, even though a later law made that act illegal (I,9).

* Tax laws shall be uniform, applying to all citizens and not putting undue burdens on a few (I,9).

* No citizen shall be officially granted an elite status over other citizens (I,9).

* The trial of all crimes except impeachment shall be by jury, and shall be held in a place where the accused has opportunity of preparing adequately for his defense (III,2).

* No one can be accused of treason for frivolous or political purposes (III,3).

- Religious freedom is guaranteed, as is the freedom of the press, of speech, of the right to assemble peaceably, and of the right to petition the government for a redress of grievances (Amendment I).

- The right to keep and bear arms shall not be infringed (Amendment II).

- Soldiers shall not be arbitrarily billeted in citizens' homes (Amendment III).

- Citizens cannot be unreasonably searched or seized or their papers taken from their persons or in their homes (Amendment IV).

- No one can be forced to testify against himself (Amendment V).

- Citizens have the right to a speedy trial and to have the assistance of legal counsel (Amendment VI).

- Excessive bail cannot be required, nor cruel or unusual punishment administered (Amendment VII).

- Any powers not specifically delegated to the government are reserved to the people (Amendment X).

- Slavery and involuntary servitude is abolished (Amendment XIII).

- All citizens have the right to vote (Amendment XV and XIX) without paying local poll taxes (Amendment XXIV).

What a roster of liberties! Over the past two hundred years legislation and judicial opinion have strengthened and expanded our liberties. Little wonder, then, that millions have come to America in search of political freedom. They came from the terrors of a revolutionary France, from the colonial and sectarian oppression of Ireland, from the turmoil of a Germany in rebellion, from an Italy torn by civil strife; and more recently, they came from the aftermath of the Russian Revolution, from the horror of Nazi rule and concentration camps, and from today's strifes ranging from the Caribbean and Central America to the Middle East and Southeast Asia.

★ BICENTENNIAL FIREWORKS. A display of fireworks highlighted the Bicentennial Celebration of the world's oldest democratic republic on July 4, 1976. For over two

centuries, the revolutionary dreams of our Founding Fathers have become firmly rooted in the American experience.

The Quest for Freedom of Opportunity

America is a bountiful nation. Stretching across a fertile continent and nurtured by a temperate climate. There is food and there is work. There is opportunity to try new ventures and to build new businesses. Millions came through Castle Garden and Ellis Island to seek a place for themselves and their families in this land of bounty. Driven by hunger or a chance to earn a decent living, they came. Attracted by the opportunity for a free education and the possibility of enhancing their children's future, they came.

It is a familiar story repeated in family after family of immigrants. The parents arrive, work hard and raise their children usually under harsh conditions. Their children then go on to elementary and secondary schools and jobs that improve their own family's circumstances. Finally, the grandchildren go on to college and perhaps graduate school, and from there enter the mainstream and beyond of American economic life. And throughout this process of

★ CASTLE GARDEN. Millions came through Castle Garden and Ellis Island to seek a place for themselves and their families in this land of bounty.

social and economic Americanization, there still remain strong forces preserving personal and cultural ties within the family's ethnic and religious heritage.

In America, tradition does not stifle one's progress: The way is open for someone to try something new. What a person can do counts for more than who his or her parents were, or whether he or she went to a certain school or belongs to a certain group. An immigrant can become Secretary of State, or president of a distinguished university, or a founder of a major high technology corporation. She can create an entire school of American dance, or he can start what is now the nation's largest bank. Although immigrants are prohibited by the Constitution from being President of the United States, any other position in the nation in government or industry can be theirs; nor is the presidency closed to the child of an immigrant.

Such upward mobility has been true for entire ethnic groups of immigrants. Voting power has made politics the key avenue for advancement. The Irish vote in Massachusetts, the Italian vote in Brooklyn, the Jewish vote in New York, the Polish vote in Chicago, and the Black vote in numerous cities have profoundly enhanced the fortunes of these groups and have provided the nation with talented leaders from every background. The newest immigrant groups—Hispanics and Asians from many countries from Pakistan to Korea—are likewise securing their livelihoods, sending their children to school, and beginning to learn how to participate in the political system with concerted action. Thus, the American story of assimilation over a two- or three-generation period without losing touch with family roots will be reenacted once again, and the American Dream continues.

A Time for Rededication

Liberty in America is strong. It is strong enough to fight a War of Independence. It is strong enough to cross oceans and continents. It is strong enough to provide prosperity and happiness to her citizenry. It is strong enough to resolve great social and racial injustices in her midst.

And yet, liberty in America is fragile: fragile enough to have endured slavery for eight decades; fragile enough to have permitted the economic oppression of the newly arrived immigrants. Liberty in America is fragile enough to be threatened by selfish exploitation, and fragile enough to languish because of indifference or forgetfulness.

Liberty is everyone's business. It is everyone's abiding concern. It is not the special preserve of the statesman or the warrior. Whenever we fail to exercise our liberty, our liberty dies a little from disuse. Whenever we use liberty as license to trample on the rights of others, it is our own rights and our own liberty that are wounded.

"O beautiful for patriot dream . . . ."

Whenever we turn a blind eye to the abuse of liberty by others, it is we who lose our way in the never-ending search for liberty. Eternal vigilance is the only sure guardian of our liberties.

Nearly one hundred years ago, Katherine Lee Bates wrote a hymn that aptly and poignantly expresses the American experience of liberty. It is a testament to liberty won; it is a vision of liberty embraced; and it is a prayer for a liberty that is enduring:

> O beautiful for spacious skies,
>   For amber waves of grain,
> For purple mountain majesties
>   Above the fruited plain!
>   America! America!
>   God shed His grace on thee
> And crown thy good with brotherhood
>   From sea to shining sea!
>
> O beautiful for pilgrim feet,
>   Whose stern, impassioned stress
> A thoroughfare for freedom beat
>   Across the wilderness!
>   America! America!
>   God mend thine every flaw,
> Confirm thy soul in self-control,
>   Thy liberty in law!
>
> O beautiful for heroes proved
>   In liberating strife,
> Who more than self their country loved,
>   And mercy more than life!
>   America! America!
>   May God thy gold refine
> Till all success be nobleness
>   And every gain divine!
>
> O beautiful for patriot dream
>   That sees beyond the years
> Thine alabaster cities gleam
>   Undimmed by human tears!
>   America! America!
>   God shed His grace on thee
> And crown thy good with brotherhood
>   From sea to shining Sea!

"From sea to shining sea!"